MAKING CUSTOMERS COUNT

For a complete list of Management Books 2000 titles,
visit our web-site at http://www.mb2000.com

MAKING CUSTOMERS COUNT

David Clutterbuck
Susan Kernaghan

2000

*This guide is dedicated to the station manager who, learning
that I had waited fifteen minutes to buy a ticket and had missed
my train, remonstrated: "It doesn't matter if you have to wait
half an hour or longer, you can't pay on the train!"*

First edition published 1991
New edition published 1994

This new edition published 2001 by Management Books 2000 Ltd
Cowcombe House,
Cowcombe Hill,
Chalford,
Gloucestershire GL6 8HP
Tel. 01285-760722 Fax: 01285-760708
e-mail: MB2000@compuserve.com

Printed and bound in Great Britain by printondemand-worlwide.com, Peterborough

British Library Cataloguing in Publication Data is available

ISBN 1-85252-109-0

CONTENTS

ACKNOWLEDGEMENTS

Introduction and Action Guide: Dr David Clutterbuck.

With research and contributions by Gareth Aspinall, Pauline Blakemore, Drew Erskine, Simon Rigby and Deborah Snow, and consultancy assistance from Bernard Wynne.

Additional editorial work by Nancy Marten.

Special thanks to Dr Robert Ball of the Stirling University Business School.

INTRODUCTION

If This is the Era of the Service Economy, Why is Service So Awful?

Although many companies claim to have customer-care programmes, the vast majority are, at best, partially successful.
They plateau, falling victim to the innate apathy of large
organisations. They either leave customers scarcely aware that
improvements have been made or raise their expectations to
the extent that the organisation's credibility is impaired rather
than enhanced, because the promise is not delivered. Ask the
man or woman in the street for examples of poor service and
he or she will rattle off the names of organisations that are
spending millions on customer care – banks, British Rail
('We're getting there' – we'll come back for the passengers, if
we remember), the major garage chains, the Post Office or
British Telecom.

Two things stand out from these examples. First, they are all
service businesses and therefore, in theory, ought to know
better. Second, all of them (and BT in particular) have made
significant improvements and have a commitment at top management levels to continuing to do so.

A large hotel chain has two hotels in the same town. One is
old-fashioned, a bit tatty, and has musical pipes that would do
justice to the Albert Hall. It always has 90 per cent-plus occupancy. The other is modern, with a swimming pool and

excellent facilities, yet it has trouble achieving more than 70 per cent occupancy. The difference? It's in the genuineness of the receptionist's smile, the fact that the staff go out of their way to be accommodating – in short, excellence of service.

It is not easy to create the customer-oriented organisation. Any company that aims to become customer-oriented has to overcome a number of barriers, among them:

- misconceptions of what is involved

  Typical of many companies' approach is the line taken by a clearing bank, where the initiative for a customer-care programme came from a bright personnel manager, who sold the idea to the chief executive. Several million pounds of training later, executives are wondering why nothing appears to have changed. There are two main reasons for this failure. The first is that no one thought through clearly what the objectives of the programme were, or how they would measure success if they achieved it. The second is that a customer-care programme is not the same as customer orientation. The customer-care campaign and training programme are only part (and a late part at that) of a much broader programme of change that reconstructs the whole organisation and the way it does things around the customer and his or her needs. Such a broad strategy will, in most cases, require a much higher investment, for a much longer term, and will affect every single activity within the organisation. Indeed, by viewing customer care as a campaign or programme, the bank immediately restricted what it could achieve. Customer orientation is a continuous process.

- organisational inertia

  The bigger and more bureaucratic the organisation, the tougher the task of making it customer-oriented. It may require a near-complete change of culture – something that can often be achieved only by replacing key people at multiple points in the structure. It takes time to identify what has to change, who is genuinely working to make change happen and who is simply paying lip service; to reinforce the message again and again until new attitudes and behaviours stick; and to remould the organisation so that it can continue to change in line with customers' needs, but ever more rapidly.

- public perception

Major improvements in one area, such as telephone availability, do not change public attitudes overnight. Rather, people transfer their frustration to other aspects of the service. It takes a lot of successive improvements for people to start talking about how much better an organisation is and to recognise that it is genuinely concerned to provide excellent service.

Until that point, public perception can be both a stimulus to and a drag on progress. It is a stimulus in that negative publicity forces executive action faster and more decisively than truckloads of internal reports and memoranda. But it is a drag in that people within the organisation absorb something of the public image. In perceiving their company as a poor service organisation, they inevitably think and behave to some extent in line with that image. Once the public perception becomes more positive, however, the engine of customer orientation rapidly picks up steam. Even the customers themselves start volunteering constructive suggestions, rather than complaints.

The number of companies which have got to that point in their service relationships is very few. Most of those in the case studies in this book have progressed sufficiently to understand that they still have a long way to go. Moreover, the goal posts keep moving. What is an acceptable level of service today may be hopelessly inadequate tomorrow, as customers' requirements and perceptions change.

The concept of Positive Gap Management (PGM) is useful here. Basically, it involves developing strategies for constantly keeping one step ahead of customer expectations (too far ahead and you risk alienating as much as by being too far behind). PGM is one area where total quality and customer care become inextricably linked – the perceptions of product and of service must both be positive to maintain customer loyalty.

Within the case studies presented here we hope you will discover ideas and lessons to improve the effectiveness of your drive to customer orientation. But first we provide a framework to help you ensure that your customer-oriented strategy will be effective and assess what these case-study companies have done.

One of the benefits of the 'quality revolution' is that we now expect to buy products that work and continue to work – and our expectations are usually met. That was certainly not the case fifteen years ago, in home electronics, motor vehicles and a whole range of high-profile goods. Will we, in fifteen years' time, be able to say that we receive superb service most of the time from most suppliers?

Part I
CUSTOMER CARE

1

WHAT IS CUSTOMER CARE?

One of the interesting experiments any manager can try out with his or her subordinates or colleagues is simply to ask them to define customer care. I have done this with numerous audiences, often all drawn from the same company. With very rare exceptions, the audience responds with a wide spectrum of definitions and descriptions. The exceptions are almost always in companies where the jargon of total quality (and occasionally the practice) has taken hold. Yet when questioned about the relationship between quality and customer care, even most of these people admit that they have never thought about it.

In most part, those descriptions that do not derive from total-quality training are based upon personal perception – what customer care means for the individual. Relatively few people define it in terms of benefits to, and behaviour of, the organisation. This is hardly surprising. Most of the relevant experience we can bring to bear on customer-care issues comes from the way we ourselves have been treated or mis-treated as customers.

Customer care involves a complex series of relationships between customers, individual employees and the organis-ation. But its primary focus is the customer. So how *do* we define customer care?

Service is where the transaction makes the customer feel you are a good business to do business with.

Or to put it another way:

Service is what makes your customers happy to come back.

Clearly, these definitions have a lot in common with total quality, which is normally defined as 'satisfying the customer's needs'. The difference, however, is that quality is concerned primarily with the right product at the right time; customer care with the nature of the customer relationship and the management of the interactions between the company and its customers. For example, it is possible to have products of superb quality, but to have disgruntled customers because the switchboard operator is rude and unhelpful or the accounts department makes frequent errors.

Total quality and customer care make use of many similar techniques, particularly in team-based problem-solving. However, total quality is almost entirely about systems and procedures, with the aim of producing consistency, while customer care, although it also requires considerable changes to systems and procedures, is primarily a means of establishing customer-supportive attitudes and behaviour. Its aim is not so much consistency (though a level of consistency is essential) as controlled flexibility.

It is not surprising, then, that so many companies which have embarked upon total-quality programmes have subsequently launched customer-care programmes as well.

Why Does Customer Care Matter?

The reasons companies give for embarking on customer-care programmes vary considerably. In our case studies, for example, the most common reasons were competitive pressures and the need to achieve differentiation in increasingly commoditised markets. Some saw it as a natural development of existing service-related programmes; some as a means of creating or reinforcing corporate culture; and others had been drawn to customer care as a result of growing numbers of complaints or the loss of a major customer, or by a mixture of these reasons.

In general, the reasons for starting a programme tend to include some or all of the following:

- **a need to achieve sustainable competitive advantage**

  Achieving competitive advantage isn't that difficult. Sustaining competitive advantage is tough, because most things that one company can do easily, others can usually copy with equal or greater facility. So new technology, new suppliers, different advertising and so on can usually provide only a brief respite. When the first banks introduced automatic teller machines (ATMs), for example, they justified the heavy cost in terms of customer satisfaction. But as competitors followed suit, they had to put in more terminals, and more again, at a massive cost that brought few operational benefits to their organisations. Now almost every bank has ATMs and many are interlinked to allow customers to take money from any of several networks, so that the competitive advantage is greatly diminished, if it remains at all. Worse still, the banks find that the ATMs now provide one of the most frequent causes of customer dissatisfaction – expectations have been raised that can be fulfilled only by more frequent topping up of the cash reserves in each machine and by providing more machines and more and more services.

  Customer care is an attractive alternative method of achieving competitive advantage because it is so difficult to do well. Those companies that succeed have to put in vast amounts of effort over a long period of time, creating an organisation and climate that not only make a high standard of customer care possible, but make anything less unthinkable. It takes a long time for the effects of this kind of change to be absorbed into public perception – a minimum of five years for companies of any size, in our observation. That's much longer than the lead time for almost any other form of competitive advantage you can name. None the less, there are substantial short-term benefits – in employee morale, efficiency and productivity.

- a need to put momentum behind a total-quality programme

Sooner or later, effective total quality management programmes run into the problem that most customer complaints are to do with the quality of service. Trying to tackle these issues as if they were the same as ordinary quality problems often doesn't work – how do you set measurable standards for sincerity and friendliness, for example? Customer care can be regarded as the next stage in evolution towards the customer-oriented company. The quality *mind-set* is equally applicable to customer care, but the approach and applications may differ.

Manufacturing companies tend to start with total quality management (TQM), then move on to customer care when the main processes in the logistics chain are under control.

Service-based companies typically start with customer care, then recognise the need for total-quality techniques to support their initiatives.

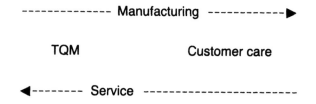

- a battle standard for change

For the chief executive who has to make radical changes in the way his or her organisation functions, a clear and stimulating vision is vital. The trouble is that many of the goals that make up top management's vision for the company may have little or no meaning or appeal to the employees as a whole. The one thing that the vast majority of employees can subscribe to both rationally and emotionally is looking after the customers. Most people instinctively feel that is the right thing to do. Customer care, therefore, provides a unifying vision around which the chief executive can build the other changes he or she must make.

- an understanding that tomorrow's business structures will be different from today's

In particular, tomorrow's business structures will emphasise flexibility of response to change in the external environment. The most significant aspect of change is in the composition, character and needs of markets, or, more precisely, of customers. As product and service differentiation become increasingly important elements of marketing, companies have little option but to get closer to their customers and to re-create their organisations, systems and behaviour around customer needs. Moreover, this is not a one-off change. Responding to customer needs will require constant minor alterations to structure and these will, to a large extent, have to happen independently of the centre, if only because obtaining approval from above would introduce delays unacceptable to customers. And from time to time the sheer volume of minor changes will demand a convulsive remaking of the organisation to fit the emerging new patterns of response required.

Some of these reasons apply equally well to public-sector bodies as to commercial and industrial organisations. Indeed, some of the most inspiring examples of customer care (as well as some of the worst neglect) can be traced to agencies such as local councils. The Borough of Richmond, for example, conducts frequent surveys to find out what Community Charge payers think of a wide range of council services, from street cleaning to meals on wheels, and uses the information to plan improvements. The school-meals service of North Yorkshire won a National Marketing Award in 1989 because it paid the children, who are its customers, the compliment of listening to them. It then designed a meals service that met their needs – with healthy food that was good value for money and was presented in an environment comparable to what they would encounter when eating out – and promoted the concept of a balanced diet. The proportion of children using the service doubled in a year; the service saved £100,000 a year and created 100 new jobs in an area of relatively high unemployment.

The one element common to all organisations we have observed successfully orienting themselves to their customers' needs is that they *think customer service*. Customer care in these organisations is not an add-on, the latest passing bright idea from management, to be obeyed rather than embraced, observed for the while rather than absorbed into the soul. It is a natural, unobtrusive and inviolable part of the way of doing business for people at all levels in the organisation. Indeed, in the most successful organisations employees often cannot see what all the fuss is about – what other acceptable way of doing business could there possibly be?

2

A TYPICAL CUSTOMER-CARE
PROGRAMME

The cases reported here are a cross-section of some of the best schemes introduced into British companies so far. Most of the companies admit readily that they have only started on their journey to customer orientation; the further they go, the more they appreciate how much ground they have to cover to achieve their objective. Yet we can draw on these organisations to identify a typical programme pattern that involves some or all of the following six common elements, as defined by the Institute of Personnel Management (IPM):

1. Decide the objectives and structure of the programme

   This is where top management should establish what the programme is supposed to achieve and outline its own role in making that happen. In practice, many schemes have been instituted with very hazy objectives and little understanding at top-management level as to what they must do to make the programme one of genuine culture change rather than of bending with the wind.

2. Audit the current situation

   The organisation attempts, usually through market research, to find out what its customers think of the quality of service provided, both in absolute terms and vis-à-vis the customer. It also looks internally, asking employees what they consider would be most unsettling for the customer in doing business with their departments.

3. Planning the programme

This is frequently carried out in workshops that can also present useful opportunities for team-building and for some problem-solving that will provide visible initial successes.

4. Defining policies and objectives

This should occur at an early stage of planning and involves looking at some of the most obvious barriers to customer care – for example, hiring procedures that do not include vetting people's attitudes towards customer service.

5. Preparing the ground

In effect, this is internal marketing. In general, the bigger the change in culture and behaviour required, the greater the cynicism the employees will exhibit. To overcome that cynicism, top management has to communicate its intentions strongly and with conviction. If employees are to give their support, they must understand why the programme is being introduced and what their role will be; they must also be convinced that the resources (particularly management time and commitment) will be made available to do the job.

6. The training programme

According to the IPM: 'There are two main schools of thought as to how this should be structured. The first holds that employees should be divided into "streams", with separate sessions for managers, supervisors, etc. The second favours the adoption of "vertical slicing", with all levels of staff attending the same courses.

'The case for "streaming" is strengthened if different messages need to be got through to different levels of management. It is also argued that, if managers are put through customer-care training first and begin acting on what they have learned, that will reinforce the subsequent training for those they are managing.

'The advantage of "vertical slicing" is that it gives staff who are not in regular contact with customers a better chance to see their job in the context of the total picture.

'Whatever approach is adopted, the aim always has to be to enable staff to see their job as part of a whole and to understand the contribution made by others in the organisation.'

Many schemes also have some mechanisms to keep the momentum going – for example, a regular newsletter illustrating successful cases of customer care in practice within the organisation.

What should happen thereafter is that the organisation slips into a constant and virtuous cycle of improvement. What actually happens in most cases is that the engine runs out of steam. Top management finds it increasingly difficult to invest a high proportion of its time beating the customer-care drum. As it slackens off, middle managers are only too glad to 'get back to normal' on the grounds that they, too, have lots of other things to do with their time. Without the visible commitment from these two layers of management, no radical changes in the direction of customer care occur, so the employees themselves lose heart – after all, nothing fundamental has changed. In some companies, the form of customer care is taken on board in some of the routines of daily management, but rare indeed is the company where the substance, too, becomes part of 'the way we do things here'.

3

WHY DO SO MANY CUSTOMER-CARE SCHEMES FAIL?

Let's be clear here what we mean by failure. Few schemes that we have observed have been total catastrophes, but equally few have been clear successes.

To judge how well a programme has performed we need a measurement. Unfortunately, many schemes have been started without thought of what success would look like or how it would be evaluated. While it might be unwarranted to assume that these must perforce have been failures, it would be equally unreasonable to regard them as successes unless the organisation has undergone a radical and positive transformation towards customer orientation. This is manifestly not the case for many of the companies we have observed.

It is easier to measure the success rate of those that did have clear objectives. What we find here is that most programmes do have short-term successes, but that the organisation finds it difficult to sustain the cycle of improvement. As the early experiments with quality circles found, once the easy improvements were made, everyone either lost interest or diverted their attention to other, more pressing, priorities, rather than step back and deal with the big issues. And yet it is tackling the big issues that will normally provide most benefits in terms of sustainable competitive advantage. In both total quality and customer care, it is becoming increasingly clear that the early tinkerings, valuable as they may be, represent only a small proportion of the benefits that could be gained if the company were prepared to remake itself entirely around its customers.

Some time ago I suggested that these companies perceive customer care as a two-stage (or more) process, in which the standard programme, largely oriented to training 'them' rather than changing 'us', was Stage I. Tackling Stage II in the same manner as Stage I is doomed to disappointment, for the following reasons:

- Stage I is aimed primarily at changing the behaviour of operators, shop assistants and other people in regular customer contact. Stage II strikes at issues these people cannot normally influence, because they are interdisciplinary, require high-level decisions or are enmeshed in organisational politics. Training in statistical process control and other operational problem-solving techniques does not prepare people for removing major organisational and cultural barriers to change.

- The majority of approaches are prescriptive, packaged solutions, which are simply too inflexible to be 'owned' by the employees and managers.

- Trying to change the culture too rapidly, without selling the benefits adequately, creates covert resistance. This subversion may not be noticeable in Stage I, when no one's territory is threatened. The politicking begins in earnest when people realise top management is seriously committed to escalating the programme.

- Top-management effort becomes diluted. Having made Stage I work, top management now feels it is time to focus on other urgent problems. Unfortunately, this is just when the customer-care programme most needs visible attention and commitment from above.

Stage II is far harder than Stage I, because it reaches into more fundamental areas of the organisation – into management style, organisation structure and systems. If Stage I is a revolution at the customer interface, Stage II is a revolution in the backrooms, where the really tough task of fulfilling customer needs takes place.

Customer-care and total-quality management programmes have to start as top-down exercises. This is essential to provide examples and role models, to ensure overall direction and commitment from the top and to enforce the level of training and participation required to make the programme a success.

Stage II, however, needs to be driven from all directions – downwards, upwards and horizontally. People at the bottom need to become much more involved in gathering the information that leads to action. Some of this action may be within their own span of control; much will lie outside their control and will have to be actioned from above. An effective approach combines general initiatives from above as to areas where top management would like people to focus continuous improvement activities, with pressure from below from people who want to see their ideas implemented. This pressure falls most heavily on the middle manager, whose role needs to change from paper-pusher and distorter of information up and down the hierarchy, to facilitator for both ends of the hierarchy. No matter how much initial gloss is put on the front-line operator, the real culture of the company will always wear through.

To play this role, the middle manager, in turn, has to put pressure on his or her peers to make things happen, becoming less of a department manager and more of a multifunctional team player.

It was Dr Deming who suggested first that 85 per cent of quality problems are created by managers. This damning record is due in part to poor technical competence, in part to lack of ability to handle people and in part to simple lack of confidence in their own ability to be genuine champions of change. Stage II of customer care requires a radical reappraisal of the role of managers at all levels. In particular, it demands that they abandon the traditional 'controlling' style of management (in which subordinates are there to help the manager do his or her job) in favour of an enabling style (in which the manager is there to help his or her subordinates do their job of satisfying the customer's needs).

To maintain this commitment a much larger proportion of the managers have to learn how to be leaders too. That doesn't come easy. Leadership involves deep responsibility at an emotional as well as an intellectual level – something whole generations of managers have learned to avoid like the plague, often with implicit approval from their boards.

The difference between the two stages is illustrated by a recent experience with an airline:

> Fifteen minutes after turning on the call light, the drinks trolley rolled up. 'Did you want anything, sir?' said the steward. I refrained from pointing out that that was why the light was on, or making a sarcastic comment such as, 'I thought you might like to know you lost an engine a few hundred miles ago.' Instead, I explained that my in-flight dinner had an extra guest – an unidentifiable insect in the dessert course. By now another steward had arrived. 'Oh dear, we can't have that, sir,' said both in unison, flashing teeth in a quick smile and racing to opposite ends of the plane to bring me a new meal each.
>
> I pointed out that it was natural to lose one's appetite in such circumstances and that all I really wanted was for them to send the offending (and hopefully dead) creature to the labs for analysis and identification. One steward was by now deflated – the customer-care charm school had not covered this situation. The other had obviously been to more advanced classes. He turned on the 'jolly them on' approach – make a joke of it, humour the chap, whatever you do, don't let him know you think he's an awkward bastard. It rapidly became clear that he intended to tip the specimen into the rubbish bag as soon as he was safely out of sight.

This was an airline that has been using its customer-care programme as the keystone of its promotion and has, it must be admitted, had enormous success in turning sullen, unhelpful staff into some of the most pleasant in the business. Indeed, they have become remarkably adept at drawing understanding smiles from customers as they apologise for the latest operational disaster.

It's all very British, this smiling in adversity. But it highlights a basic problem with the first generation of customer-care programmes: no matter how well you teach people to smile, no matter how pleasant and unfluffable they learn to be, it cannot in the end compensate for failures in the systems and procedures. Had the stewards in the example above been trained in solving problems rather than sympathising with passengers, they would have understood that the priorities were to:

- reassure the passenger that the intruder was almost certainly harmless, but they would make sure it was checked out;

- take my name and address, so that I could subsequently be fully reassured (or told to visit the nearest hospital for obscure tropical diseases as rapidly as possible).

There is a great danger in many sectors of industry that customer care may become synonymous in the public mind with superficiality; that it is perceived to be as plastic as the in-flight catering. Many companies which have invested heavily in the first stage of customer care – from retailing to electronics, financial services to automobile manufacture – are conscious that their programmes have slowly but surely plateaued as the easy problems are resolved. The problem is that no one remembers how awful things used to be. Their expectations are based on the best of what happens now. When performance drops below the current best, they are not unnaturally and perhaps quite rightly disgruntled by standards that would have delighted them a couple of years ago.

It isn't surprising that companies allow this to happen. There really are other priorities to pursue. The trick is to stick with customer care long enough and seriously enough for it to free up the time you need to deal with these other priorities. It isn't adequate to revisit customer care on an occasional or at-need basis. Yet a lot of companies expect to do just that.

The problem with these companies is that they simply haven't taken on board exactly what customer care is, or how fundamentally it affects every activity within the organisation. A perceptive article by Richard Wellins and Patterson Weaver in *Training* magazine explores some of the most common misconceptions these companies indulge in. Among them:

- 'Good customer service is a matter of knowing how to deal with complaints.'

  Companies spend millions of pounds asking people to complain to them, then fail to use the information strategically. Many don't even give the customer a satisfactory response. How many times have you used the 'happy card' in a hotel room to lambast the poor service and received no acknowledgement?

- 'If our customers are unhappy, we'd better shake up the customer-service department.'

  More relevant would be to question why the customer-service department exists at all, when everyone in the organisation should take responsibility for customer care. Making customer care a specialist job absolves other people from service responsibility.

- 'First-line people aren't paid to think; they're paid to carry out our rules.'

  In today's workforce, everybody should be paid to think. The 'primary customer interface' in most organisations is with people at the bottom of the pyramid. If they can't respond to the customer's needs, it is probably too late to provide satisfaction.

- 'High turnover prevents us from investing in customer-contact people.'

  Some business sectors, such as retail or hotels, do have high rates of labour turnover. Instead of using this as an excuse for not training people thoroughly in customer care, these businesses should ask themselves why turnover is so high. By increasing employees' self-respect, they can begin to create the concept of a career in service.

- 'Smile and the world smiles with you.'

  In a single month Wellins and Weaver received twenty brochures advertising simple, one-day training programmes for service employees – what they call 'one-shot smile training'. The problem with such approaches is that they are inevitably superficial and seen as such by employees. Companies really committed to service training spend a lot longer on the basics and reinforce them with rigorous on-the-job training by supervisors and managers thereafter.

  Some of the 'packaged' customer-care programmes we have observed make use of behavioural modelling to try to change people's behaviour. But there is little evidence that this new behaviour will stick unless people really want it to and believe it is fully supported by the organisation. As an article in *Personnel Management* expressed it:

  > 'In the service sector this had been the traditional training approach; it attempts to gain a direct adoption of certain supposedly ideal types of behaviour. At its worst it reduces to a parrot-style "have a nice day" as a veneer on indifference. At its best it embodies a truthful – if at times unwelcome – attempt to communicate the standards of behaviour that customers appreciate, but in isolation it still tends to fail to recognise the private reality of the people called upon to change their behaviour. It begs the question "what's in it for me?".'

- 'Examples of heroism are enough to change service behaviour.'

  War stories of exceptional feats of customer care do have their value in creating a customer-oriented climate. But on their own they have little effect, because for most people these opportunities to become customer-service heroes are few and far between. The real heroes are people who perform exceptional service day in, day out – the people your customers (and you) know they can depend on.

In sum, therefore, the main reason customer-care schemes fail is that the organisation does not enter them with a full appreciation of and commitment to the scale of change that will be required. Of course, change is not comfortable, frequent change is even less so and frequent radical change can be downright painful. But like any form of exercise, after a while those sore and painful muscles gradually toughen up and most people can actually come to enjoy it.

Successful service excellence initiatives start with a clearly defined vision of customer needs, both now and in the future, and of how to build a profitable business through satisfying those needs.

Many companies miss out this stage, thereby losing the benefits of focusing everyone's attention on clear goals. Many companies also fall at the next hurdle – they move straight into awareness training for staff at the customer interface, on the assumption that they can change attitudes and therefore behaviour. This almost never succeeds.

Successful initiatives recognise that the organisation must change first. In particular, its structures, systems and standards must all be seen by the employees to be undergoing change in line with the customer vision, so that attitude and behaviour changes will be supported in the workplace environment.

The customer vision

- Research
- Defined customer needs
- Strategy

Structure

Systems

Standards

Attitudes

Behaviour

4

ORGANISING AN EFFECTIVE CUSTOMER-CARE PROGRAMME

Although in the previous chapter we talked in terms of a second stage of customer care, this really applies only to those organisations that have already introduced a programme and now need to prevent it from plateauing and going the way of most other management fads. The culture of an organisation is usually remarkably resistant to such invasions of ideas and attitudes, treating them much like viruses. The foreign bodies are absorbed, then gradually isolated and enclosed until they wither and recede of their own accord. Then the organisation carries on much as before.

It would have been better in many cases had these organisations spent longer in preparation and in thinking through exactly what they wanted to achieve, before they launched. For some companies, however, lengthy preparation time was not a luxury available. British Airways, for example, was in a race for survival when it started its programme. To some extent, the recognition by everyone in the company that this was a crisis, and that top management was totally committed to using customer service as the way out of trouble, overcame the lack of preparation time. Now, as the first flush wears off, BA is having to step back and look more closely at the fundamentals of what it intends to achieve.

The Customer-Oriented Vision

The whole process of customer care has to start with a vision – a vision of what a truly customer-oriented company would ideally look like in a particular industry sector. For example, a fully customer-oriented airline would aim to reduce the hassle of travelling to a minimum. It is always a puzzle that, while travel is supposed to be fun and while people spend most of their time sitting down, almost all long-distance travellers arrive tired and irritable. An obvious – although debatable – conclusion is that their arrival state has something to do with how they are treated at the airport and in flight. So obvious, in fact, that that is exactly what many travellers conclude.

A totally hassle-free travelling environment would include all of the following. Not one is beyond the bounds of technology or the bounds of either the airlines or the airport authorities:

- automatic seat allocation when the ticket is purchased;

- collection of luggage at the terminal entrance (common at US airports), or at bus/train stations within the airport, thus considerably reducing the amount of tiresome dragging of personal effects and the congestion in the terminals;

- coding of luggage labels to deliver each passenger's batch of luggage in one go;

- a secure conveyor system to transport luggage that has been through customs directly to the car park or to the bus/train station;

- preplanned arrangements for helping passengers of all ticket classes relax through flight delays (e.g. facilities where they can watch television, exercise, do business, or simply sleep);

- a reasonably wide choice of in-flight menu and wines up to twenty-four hours before the flight, by returning a reply-paid card that arrives with the ticket.

And so on. One of the most useful exercises I conduct with boards of directors, and with people at other levels within an organisation, is to ask them to visualise the *worst* things they could do to their customers: if you really want to ensure that someone doesn't use your company again, what do you have to do to them?

Two things usually emerge from this exercise. One is a realisation (after customer surveys) that the organisation actually does do many, perhaps most, of these things from time to time. The other is a list of opposites, of things that ideally the customer would expect and recognise as good service. This list makes a starting-point for the vision of the truly customer-oriented company. The vision is gradually built up and enhanced by gathering information from four key sources:

1. The customers themselves

Every customer has feelings about how he or she should be treated. But their expectations are usually somewhat lower. Part of the information-gathering exercise involves identifying the gap between the customer's ideal and his or her expectations, and where the customer perceives your company and your competition within that gap.

There is a further point often worth measuring – the technically possible ideal service. People's imaginations of the ideal are often limited by their experience so far. But it is often possible to redesign a product or service fundamentally to make it meet the customer's needs far more closely than he or she could have imagined. How many people, for example, would have thought of defining their ideal television unit as one which allowed them to store any programme they could not watch when it was broadcast? Yet very few people in Britain would now envisage having a television without a video attachment.

Identifying the three benchmarks of service – the customer's expected level of service, the customer's perception of the ideal service and the technically possible ideal service

– allows you to assess your relative competitive position in service excellence terms. Focusing on the two upper levels reveals opportunities to make major improvements rather than successive incremental improvements – and thus to leapfrog other companies with a perceived higher service quality.

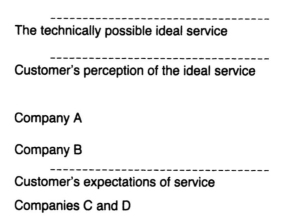

The initial gathering of information from customers should be through a controlled survey. We usually recommend a two-stage approach: a postal questionnaire, accompanied by an explanatory letter from the chief executive, emphasising the importance of the information to the customer as well as to the organisation; and a telephone survey, where comments can be followed up in depth.

This activity provides statistical data that enable top management to prioritise both 'irritant points' and opportunities to add customer value. The postal survey is particularly valuable in assessing frequency of an irritant, the telephone survey in weighting it in terms of importance. In-person interviews with customers can provide an additional, qualitative evaluation of where the company stands now in terms of customer service.

All of this information is valuable, because it provides a basis for measuring improvement year on year. But it really is only a starting-point, for three reasons:

- it is a very broad-brush measure, useful mainly for strategic purposes

  For monitoring changes in the nitty gritty of operations, much more focused, detailed measurements will normally be required.

- customers' perceptions of service are just one indication of customer orientation

  It is very easy for top management to assume that improvements in customer-satisfaction scores demonstrate that the organisation has become more customer-oriented. In reality, the organisation may not have changed. The improved customer perception may be to do with greater reliability of products (a quality rather than customer-care issue), with the behaviour of a few key individuals, whose excellence is likely already to have been recognised by headhunters, or with a change in the customers' requirements, which have moved closer to your offering. For example, in a period of high interest rates, builders are less active and it is easier for suppliers of cement, bricks and so on to deliver quickly and on time. Customer satisfaction will therefore be relatively high. As the building industry picks up again, the capabilities of the supplier companies to deliver quickly and on time may become severely stretched. Customer satisfaction will then fall. The truly customer-oriented company has systems that will ensure a high level of service in all circumstances.

- the 'intuitive factor'

  This is important in assessing what market research of this kind has to contribute. *Personnel Management* again draws upon British Airways to illustrate the point:

  > 'In 1983 British Airways, in the course of its hugely popularised efforts to recapture a value-added image, intensified its market research, trying to establish exactly what it was that made passengers

elect to fly a particular airline again – repeat purchase being a very significant factor in this industry's revenue.

'Through a perhaps more imaginative research approach than previously adopted, the airline identified a number of salient features of service for its major passenger segments. For relatively inexperienced VFR passengers (visiting friends and relations), anxiety reduction was paramount; for holiday-makers, glamour, champagne and excitement were the key; while for the experienced and perhaps jaundiced business traveller on short haul the needs were described as "rational" – a timely arrival, special communication facilities in the event of unavoidable delays and so on.

'This research certainly helped in the development of a largely successful strategy and clearly pointed to a need to promote the facets of sympathy and courtesy – the elements of the well-publicised "putting people first" campaign.

'But, sophisticated though the research was, it failed to identify one potentially salient feature for the last passenger segment, the business traveller. For in the spring of 1983 a small airline called British Midland introduced the breakfast sausage to early-morning internal flights, and bleary-eyed businessmen switched carriers in their thousands. The supposed rationality of business travellers did, of course, demand timeliness and so on, but the added value was the sausage – the cattle truck "shuttle" had been displaced. To BA's credit, it managed within months to launch the super shuttle, replete with breakfast, and its dominance was re-established.

'The moral of this story is not that BA got it wrong – to err is human – but rather that some flair is required in establishing exactly what the salient features are in identifying the "sausage factor", and in being sufficiently nimble to provide it quickly.'

The only way top management will be able to identify these nuances of need is by identifying closely with the customers themselves. In practice, this means two things:

- a great deal of personal contact with customers, preferably at the point where the service transaction takes place;

- becoming a customer as often as possible.

Personal contact

Not long ago, in an interview with the chairman and chief executive of one of Britain's largest multinational companies, I was astounded to hear him say: 'Oh, I haven't spent any time with customers since I became chairman. It's not my job.' It was no surprise to see that company's profits and share price dip sharply only a few months later.

The chief executive who is not in frequent and inquiring contact with his or her customers is missing out on the intuitive intelligence needed to pursue a customer-oriented strategy. He or she is also sending a powerful negative message to the rest of the organisation about the importance of customers. Instead, he or she should be deliberately arranging what one company has called 'humble days', when customers are met with for the specific purpose of listening.

When Sir John Sainsbury tours 100 stores a year, he does not do so just to talk to managers and staff. He wants to know what his customers think too. Only in this way can he be sure that the strategy he and his board colleagues are pursuing will meet customers' shopping needs.

The same principle should apply all the way down the line within the customer-oriented company. Every employee, from senior management to the shopfloor, who does not regularly meet customers face to face should be encouraged and have the opportunity to carry out his or her own customer research. Indeed, for managers, this must be a basic responsibility of the job.

Becoming the customer

Putting oneself in the customer's shoes is rarely easy. It requires managers to shuck off all their background knowledge of why things happen in the way they do and allow themselves simply to experience the service in the way the customer would. For example, at Scotrail, a new general manager, Chris Green, insisted that managers spend time travelling around the region with their families, second class, to experience the frustrations themselves. He also put senior managers into contact with customers by holding a radio phone-in and distributing among them the telephone numbers of all the callers who could not speak to him. The senior managers were told to spend the next day telephoning these inquirers and responding to their requests and comments.

Another powerful example of trying on the customer's shoes is given by the Swedish company Cerberus. Here's how we reported its story in *On Achieving Excellence*:

'Hans Brundin wishes more problems with security alarms he sells were caused by his company, Cerberus, in Stockholm, Sweden. But he found that nine out of 10 alarms are false, and half of those are caused by negligent handling by the customer or workers, such as carpet fitters or painters.

'The company-caused false alarms are easily and quickly fixed. "Our business mission is to give our end users 100 percent security with a 20-year guarantee," he explains. To tackle problems caused by its own staff, Cerberus developed an intensive internal training program.

'But reducing customer- or construction-worker-caused false alarms is a trickier proposition, one Brundin was determined to achieve. The company produced a training program for all operators and established a users' club to keep in touch with customers and the fire brigades. But Brundin still wasn't content. "I wanted to prove our statistics were correct," he says.

'"I went to the fire station in Stockholm, which has more false alarms than any station in Sweden, and trained as a fireman." After, Brundin went out on fire-alarm calls for a day. Out of six alarms during the day, five were unnecessary. Even the real fire was caused by people who had been working in homes.

'The day as a fireman proved Brundin's statistics. "We now have a lot more information about our customers and we better understand their problems. The next step is to expand our users' club so we can become even better informed. We now have 550 members but want to expand the club throughout Sweden," to all customers. Through local fire stations, Cerberus has tracked information on more than 5,000 alarms. The steady flow of information helps Cerberus check progress on decreasing false alarms.'

2. The employees

Whether they have been asked to gather information consistently or not, most employees have some insights into what pleases and upsets customers. It is important here, however, to differentiate between frequent small irritants to a lot of customers and the once-in-a-blue-moon unpleasant exchange with an unjustifiably irate customer. Employees' perceptions can often be coloured more by one very sour and emotionally draining incident than by a multitude of pinpricks.

3. The competition

Some time ago several experiments asked groups of managers to assess what would happen to an unnamed company's products over the next ten years, on the basis of a six-year track record of growth. Hints were dropped to one group that made them suspect that it was their own company and to another that it was one of their main competitors. Those who thought it was their company continued the growth to show an exponential increase in sales; those who thought it was the competition drew an exponential decline.

The lesson from these experiments is that managers are almost always overly optimistic about what their own organisation can do and overly pessimistic about the competition's performance. That frequently leads them to write off anything the competition does as inferior, or as a gimmick. Yet the customer-oriented company should be primed to polish up and improve upon any good idea the competition has for enhancing customer service. If it moves fast enough, the public perception of who was the innovator will be obscured. Moreover, it prevents the competitor establishing its new approach as an element of differentiation.

4. Other business sectors

Very often the most fruitful area of search for new components to the service vision is other industry sectors which have tackled similar problems in different ways. It is sometimes possible to leapfrog existing ways of doing things by borrowing concepts from completely different industries. For example, one of the best pieces of 'creative swiping' at the ITEM Group was to look at the world of complex project management, particularly in computing and construction. By adapting project-control techniques from these areas to house-magazine and annual-report publishing, we were able to define a new level of service in those markets. Some companies go to remarkable extremes to obtain customer feedback. Northwestern Mutual Life Insurance Co., reports *Fortune*, asks five policy holders to descend on company headquarters in Milwaukee for five days once a year. Their task? To tell the company what it is doing right or wrong. The customer inquisitors have access to any documentation they wish.

Their comments – warts and all – are published in the annual report.

Focus on Customer Needs

The amount of data that can be gathered by these various means is enormous. It needs to be assimilated, sorted and focused in a way that will provide the company with precise and sustainable competitive advantage. To do that, customer needs must be aggregated in a way that makes sense for strategic planning. Our own approach is to divide all the customer-service needs we can identify into three categories:

- 'hygiene factors' – elements of the service that people expect and which cause complaints if they are absent or badly handled;

- readily imitable competitive advantages – things you or your competitors could do to improve customer service, but which would not provide significant and valuable differentiation for long;

- sustainable competitive advantage – things that competitors will find it hard to imitate.

The latter are, of course, the hardest. Very often they consist not of one innovation but of a package of related innovations, some obvious, some in the back room. Competitors frequently make the mistake of trying to copy the obvious elements without understanding the framework behind them. In doing so, they may add to your company's reputation by showing how difficult it is to carry out this new element of service well.

Now top management is in a position to make some major strategic decisions about where to put its resources in order to build unassailable relationships with its customers. It is also in a position to begin remaking the entire organisation around the customer.

Customer-Oriented Change

The customer-oriented marketing strategy is the first building-block in remaking the organisation. The ultimate aim is to have an operation which responds rapidly to changing customer needs; is frequently proactive, anticipating or creating needs and having a planned approach to meeting them; and is staffed by people who *think customer service*.

At this stage it is particularly important to be clear about what changes the organisation needs to make. As we saw earlier, one of the failings with many programmes is that they assume that the objective is to change behaviour. This may be partly true, but in order to change behaviour and make the new behaviour stick, we must first change the structure, the systems, the standards and the attitudes that prevail within the organisation. All these activities can take place simultaneously, if necessary. But it is of little value – and indeed, may increase resistance from both employees and customers – to attempt to change attitudes and behaviour without first demonstrating that the internal operating environment is changing to support the new ways of working.

In effect, to create changes in thinking and behaviour at the bottom, top management must look to its own laurels. A recent study by Boston Consulting Group highlights some of the attitude changes that have to take place at this level before the process of customer-oriented change can begin. The study examined fifteen European companies 'that have been particularly successful at creating innovative customer value'. It identified four elements behind these companies' success, which it describes as beliefs, structure, process and resource allocation.

Under beliefs, the study asserted that: 'Companies successfully based on value reject the notion of commodities. There may be commodity products, but every product can be differentiated. The company must have a vision of being driven by value.' The key is for people within the company to be constantly on the look-out to differentiate their products and services by moving with the changing patterns of customer needs.

Under structure, the study points out that most organisations are built for efficiency, which is an internal measure, as opposed to value, which is an external measure. It poses two key questions for Chief Executive Officers to answer:

- Who in your company is thinking about customer value?

- Who in your company is delivering customer value?

The answers to those questions often force companies to re-evaluate the usefulness of traditional salesforces, BCG suggests.

Under process, the study identifies a ragbag of activities aimed at breaking down the barriers of functional specialisation within the company and between the company and its customers. In particular, it advocates developing products jointly with customers.

Finally, under resource allocation it questions the traditional accounting-based methods of assessing the payback on investments and suggests instead adopting procedures that give greater weight to the question of how significantly investments will contribute to customer-oriented goals.

Comparing the best and worst organisations in its study, BCG was able to draw up the following chart:

	Best Organisation	Worst Organisation
Beliefs	Every commodity product can be transformed into a value business	In commodity products we must compete on price
Structure	Product management and sales functions centred around customer value	Product management and sales functions specialised and autonomous
Process	Customer needs cut through internal specialisation	Functional procedures set up for internal efficiency
Resource Allocation	Probing for underlying customer value	Based on financials

Changing the Structure

The structure of an organisation defines how people see their responsibilities and, most importantly, how things get done through formal channels. Unless the structure supports the customer-oriented strategy, customer-care training will operate in a vacuum.

In practice, creating a customer-oriented structure means rebuilding the organisation from the customer interface up. If defined customer needs are the foundation stone, job specifications that will deliver customer satisfaction are the first layers. Each job at what we can call the primary customer interface has three components:

- roles – what people perceive they are there for; the broad outcomes they must achieve and the general manner in which they should make them happen;

- responsibilities – the specific duties they have to the customer, to other employees, to the organisation and to themselves;

- interfaces – other people who must be consulted, or who must give their support, if the employee is to fulfil his or her roles and responsibilities. Service excellence is strengthened if that support becomes a right.

There may well be overlap between these components. For example, making sure that customers do not have to queue for long can be viewed as both a role and a responsibility; similarly, checking with another department before taking action that will affect how it functions can be seen as both a responsibility and an interface. Sometimes it helps to look upon roles as having primarily an external focus, with responsibilities focused on the workings of the employee's own department and interfaces concerned with relations with others.

Whichever way companies choose to analyse each job, the aim is not precision but understanding. Once people recognise that their jobs have these components, they can begin to understand more clearly the implications for how they go about what they do. In effect, getting people to think about their jobs in this way demands answers to the following basic questions:

- What am I here to do?

- Who am I doing it for?

- Whose help do I need?

- Who needs my help?

It is remarkable how few employees at the primary customer interface have ever had to consider those questions, and even fewer have had to assign priorities to the answers. Formal job descriptions are not usually of much help, either because they are designed with operational rather than customer objectives in mind, or because the employee has no part in formulating them, or both. Yet without that understanding, how can they be expected to provide a consistently high level of customer service?

Once the employees at the primary customer interface have agreed with management on the roles, responsibilities and interfaces of their jobs, the organisation can begin building upwards. Each layer of management has three key roles:

- to support the people at the primary customer interface in delivering exactly what the customer needs;

- to control the processes so that deviations become apparent and are remedied immediately and prevented in future;

- to oil the wheels of all the customer-critical interfaces of his or her area of responsibility.

Each layer of management also has a number of key responsibilities, which include:

- to gather and disseminate information on customer needs and behaviour;
- to plan new initiatives;
- to motivate people to think customer service.

In general, any activity that does not meet these definitions is unlikely to add any value to the organisation, and the manager needs to question whether it is part of his or her job.

Systems

Systems must support the structure in delivering a product/ service mix to a consistent quality in line with the customer-oriented strategy. Most business systems have been designed to support internal needs. They can, and often do, therefore, work in direct opposition to the customer-oriented objectives.

Because customer needs will evolve over time and because on occasion delivering customer service may require an override of standard procedures, all systems in the organisation need to be built for flexibility as well as robustness. Typical of the kind of systems where this does not work are the computer billing systems used by so many utilities and large service organisations. A personal example serves to illustrate the point. Some years ago I cancelled my account with one of the leading credit-card companies. I wrote to say I would not be renewing my subscription and made sure that there was no outstanding debt to pay. But, in a cost-saving move, the company had issued cards intended to last for two years, even though subscription renewal was annual. So the computer continued to send out invoices for the next year's subscription. After a few months, it started adding interest to this sum, then sending threatening letters. After about six months, numerous letters, telephone calls and promises to correct the error, I received a curt letter to say that my account had been discontinued, with the implicit suggestion that I was a bad debt. In the same post was a letter asking if I would like a card for my wife too.

Such stories are not remarkable. Virtually everyone has their own private stock, from publishers who deliver the wrong books and keep chasing for payment months after they have been sent back, to companies that charge extra for twenty-four-hour delivery when they took a week. Nine times out of ten the hapless person who handles the complaints blames the computer. But, of course, it is the computer's fault on only the rarest of occasions. What has happened is that the system has been designed around operational needs rather than around the customer. Its rigidity means it cannot easily respond to the sorts of problem customers encounter. Had it been designed around the customer, these kinds of situation could have been foreseen and allowed for. The range of systems that influence customer service is much wider than invoicing and delivery, of course. Most, sometimes all, functions within the organisation need to come under scrutiny. Certain systems areas may need priority attention.

Operating procedures

Vast procedural manuals are normally a sign of the inflexible, bureaucratic, internally focused organisation. But written operating procedures are frequently also essential for reasons of health and safety, for consistency of service and to help new recruits get the hang of a job quickly. They can also be a valuable means of measuring performance. Three golden rules will normally help maintain a balance between bureaucracy and slackness:

- keep the rulebook short and simple, focused on the priorities

  The more rules you have, the more difficult they are to remember and the more difficult it is for people to recognise which are the important ones. And the more rules you have, the more people will let the rules, rather than the situation, guide them in what they do.

- involve employees themselves in drawing up and monitoring the procedures – and in explaining them to new recruits

  That way they will understand the spirit of the rules rather than just the letter. If you can't involve them in this way, make sure they understand the reasoning behind the rules and how they relate back to their roles, responsibilities and interfaces.

- express the rules in positive language

  This way you will be much more likely to induce positive behaviour.

Rewards

Most incentive payment systems are built around sales or profit goals. Not surprisingly, that tends to affect where people focus their effort and attention. Some companies have taken to writing in the job description a general statement about customer care as an objective of each manager and salesperson, but very few measure this aspect of their performance actively or make it a significant part of the calculations for their annual bonus or pay review.

For many organisations, customer service will come high on people's personal agenda only if it is an integral and important part of the reward system. One company that has recognised this is Rank Xerox. In 1988 it introduced a scheme for the top 135 managers in its international headquarters and European operations, whereby their annual salary review could be increased or decreased by up to 4 per cent depending on measurements of customer loyalty and satisfaction. For that year the two measurements were given equal weighting, with most of the managers involved in the UK gaining increases near the maximum. For 1989 customer loyalty received a higher weighting, at 70 per cent. The scheme has been so successful that it is being extended to all employees at Rank Xerox's international headquarters in Marlow.

A US consultancy, the Forum Corporation, identifies three levels of impact from customer feedback:

- simply informing employees what customers have to say, in a non-threatening manner;

- using customer feedback as the basis for annual or quarterly incentive schemes;

- using customer feedback as the basis for every pay packet.

As one of its consultants says: 'Your compensation system is perhaps the most long-lasting, year-in and year-out system that you have. If you want to institutionalise long-term commitment to customer service, it's hard to beat.'

Of course, the range of rewards available is much wider than money. Equally, perhaps more, important is recognition. As Terry Lunn of brewers Joshua Tetley maintains: 'The real key to improving people's performance is to continue to reward and recognise it.' Tetley recently carried out a survey of 500 people it was recruiting. When asked, 'When did you last receive reward and recognition?' 95 per cent could talk only about an experience at school. The scope for using the power of praise is enormous.

Recruitment

More and more companies are coming to recognise that their hiring systems effectively set the limits on the level of customer service they can offer. Put more simply, if you hire people with good attitudes towards the customer to begin with, you stand a much higher chance of achieving the kinds of behaviour you require. Joshua Tetley, again, uses selection research techniques to establish applicants' 'life themes' or dominant behaviour and attitudes. In particular, the company wants to know if people will be warm and friendly to customers, or shy and always finding other things to do, such as answering the telephone. Says Lunn: 'People who have got high customer orientation will want to keep winning that customer again and again; they want to keep providing excellent service. It's part of their mission in life to be good at providing good customer service.'

There are a number of techniques available for creating, monitoring and improving systems. Most suffer from being internally focused. At ITEM we have developed an approach that builds systems up from defined customer needs. This approach involves analysing exactly what existing systems do that support and hinder the delivery of customer service (and of customer needs in general). The key questions that must be asked are:

- What is the orientation of the existing systems for getting things done?

- What objectives should we set for systems, to make them customer-oriented? And how will this change them?

These objectives will normally stem from the customer needs identified earlier in the project.

Standards

Like structures and systems, standards can be either internally or externally oriented. By and large, companies set standards on internally generated criteria – for example, how many items a shop assistant should push through the computerised checkout equipment in an hour.

In the product-quality arena, there is a marked and accelerating trend for large customers to seek partnerships with smaller numbers of suppliers, who can be relied upon to produce to predetermined and strict quality criteria. Implicit in this arrangement are very clear standards specified by the customer. These standards are often essential, for example, if the customer is to operate on just-in-time principles. As yet, this trend has not greatly affected the service sectors or the service elements of manufacturing businesses. It will, however. Japanese companies, in particular, are paying increasing attention to service standards, not least as a means of raising white-collar productivity. Moreover, as companies in the West concentrate more and more on core activities, they will place increasing pressure on their service suppliers to ensure that their offerings to their own customers are not undermined by failings on the part of bought-in elements.

A recent example from ITEM's own experience illustrates the point. A client company introducing a major change programme needed some explanatory materials to hand out at meetings with managers on a Monday morning. There was just time to prepare and print the materials, which would be shipped on Sunday night to several destinations around the country. The department in charge of the project accepted the printer's assurances that the distribution would be handled competently, but didn't check which courier firm was to be used. (Had they done so, they would have uncovered a history of unreliability.) The courier delivered all the packages to one location. A full day was wasted putting matters right and placating a justifiably angry customer. The lessons the department learned were:

- never leave a key element of the process to an unknown third party;

- establish a close and direct relationship with a supplier able to provide consistently reliable service;

- develop and enforce a very clear set of standards with that supplier.

So how can we ensure that the standards employees and suppliers are operating match customer requirements? And how can we make sure that, once set, people achieve those standards?

Setting standards

Customer-oriented standards originate in the definition of customer needs. The concepts of role and responsibility describe what has to be done to meet those needs. Standards describe the manner in which those activities should be carried out.

Two key concepts are relevant here. The first is that standards are best set in collaboration with (or by) the people who have to work to them. Our experience suggests that employees who have been given the opportunity to learn at first hand what customers' needs are, tend to set higher, more realistic standards than their managers. They are also more motivated to achieve, sustain and improve those standards, because they feel ownership of them.

A useful environment for setting standards – whether for internal or external customers' needs – is a formal meeting involving members of the work group and representatives of the customer. The participants should work through each important activity or output, to ensure that the standards set against it are:

- relevant;

- challenging;

- realistic;

- measurable.

They should also establish *how* each standard will be measured.

The second problem relates to the basis of comparison. The

problem with standards set with an internal focus is that they will usually be based either upon current practice or upon customers' current expectations. To be a source of constant improvement, they need to be assessed against best practice elsewhere – in other words, to be benchmarked. In a recent publication for the Department of Trade and Industry, we argued that benchmarking should take place at four levels:

- between departments or divisions of the same firm;

- between the firm and its competitors in the same industry;

- between the firm and companies in parallel sectors of industry;

- between functions of the firm and their counterparts in completely different industries.

The benchmarking process opens up opportunities to provide levels of service that exceed customer expectations and create differentiation through service. Its basic assumption is that most activities will be handled by someone, somewhere, better than by you. If you can identify that organisation and measure what it does, you can adapt its approach to your company's needs – and your customers'.

Once set, standards need to be revised frequently. One reason for this is that customer expectations will be changed by external events, such as:

- improvements in service by competitors;

- comparison with service levels in other markets (e.g. most people find it difficult to understand why a rented television so rarely goes wrong, while rented photocopiers seem to be constantly under repair);

- gradual acceptance of your service levels as the norm.

Another reason is that it provides a continuous opportunity for involving employees, for capitalising on their pride in work.

Attitudes

Attitudes are the precursors of behaviour – behaviour changes will not stick unless people's attitudes support them. Changing attitudes is one of the most difficult tasks. You cannot force someone to change his or her attitudes. They may adjust their behaviour under threat or temptation, but their underlying attitude will remain the same and will cause their behaviour to revert as soon as the pressure is removed. People change their own attitudes as they readjust their perceptions of the world about them and their place in it.

For this reason, it is usually preferable to start by hiring people whose natural attitudes are already oriented towards customer service. For the established company, however, that is tantamount to saying, 'If I were you, I wouldn't have started from here' – and about as useful. Although better hiring practices can gradually bring about the kind of change in predominant attitudes that is required, the main priority for the present is how to change the attitudes of people already within the organisation.

So what creates customer-oriented attitudes? Critical are:

- a feeling of responsibility;

- a feeling of being valued;

- a feeling of being supported;

- an understanding of who the customers are and what they need, and of what the organisation's customer-oriented strategy is and their individual plan to achieve it.

Structure, systems and standards are behind each of these components of customer-oriented attitudes. Attitudinal change is likely to be superficial at best unless these three earlier phases are visibly underway.

A feeling of responsibility

Most people react well to being given responsibility, as long as:

- they believe they will have the resources they need to carry it out;
- they believe they have the competence (or can be trained) for it;
- they recognise the importance of the task.

A feeling of being valued

Once people believe that the task is important, they begin to grow in confidence and self-esteem. The trick is to recognise the value they add to the organisation with frequent rewards for good service. A problem with many companies' programmes is that they emphasise the achievements of people who have carried out exceptional customer service – for example, the specialist bookshop manager who helped a customer out by driving fifty miles further on his way home to deliver an urgent order. Most people don't have the opportunity to make such grand gestures. Their sense of value to the organisation can be enhanced if managers actively seek opportunities to praise them simply for doing the job well. It doesn't take much effort to write, 'Nice job, thanks,' even if you do it 100 times a day.

A feeling of being supported

While praise helps here too, the most important ingredient is an understanding by the employee's manager of what support he or she should be providing. One way of looking at this is in terms of employee rights. If the employee is to do his or her job in meeting the customer's requirements for service, then he or she has the right to certain kinds of support from his or her junior manager. The junior manager in turn has the right to certain kinds of support from his or her boss, and so on up the chain.

We advise the manager who wants his or her staff to take on responsibilities and the attitudes that go with them to start by explaining what the responsibilities are (or even better, to work with the employees to establish them); then to ask them to define what support they need. Some of it he or she may be able to supply personally (for example, 'We need to have half an hour of your time every week to talk through any problems we encounter'). Other support needs may involve other departments or external suppliers. As we saw earlier, the manager's role is in part to oil the wheels of these interfaces, to make sure his or her staff do receive the support they need. The manager must be prepared to listen to and accept their criticisms when the required support is not forthcoming – which is perhaps the toughest part of all.

Understanding

Because attitudes are developed from perceptions, the most effective way of changing them is to enable people to adjust their perceptions. That means feeding them information and allowing them opportunities to acquire information for themselves. At first, they will normally filter or adapt the information they receive according to their existing prejudices. Eventually, however, the volume of information that contradicts their perceptions forces a gradual reappraisal. Instant, overnight conversions are unlikely, but it is not unusual to see hardened cynics become, over time, the most fervent champions of customer care.

How can you provide this form of information? One of the most important methods is to tell people and keep telling them, again and again. Use any and every medium – the company newspaper, video, sales meetings, articles in the external media (employees believe messages far more readily if they are announced to the outside world as well) and, most important of all, face to face. The first hurdle is to convince them that you mean what you say – most employees have a remarkable reserve of cynicism about management initiatives. Think of this cynicism as callouses, built up over years of bitter experience as a protective layer; to overcome it you will have to get under the skin.

One way of doing so is to create opportunities where people can learn for themselves rather than be told by you. For example, let them carry out customer research. They will believe what they find themselves far more easily than the data they receive in a memo from above. Moreover, the attitudes and perceptions they encounter outside will often be sufficiently unexpected to make them step back and reappraise their own.

What will often convince people most, though, is to see real change happening that supports them in their roles and responsibilities towards the customer. It is at this point that their attitudes either have to change or come into open conflict with the requirements of their job. There is no longer any excuse for not having good customer-service attitudes. Particularly if their performance is measured in customer-service terms, the pressure on these people to change will increase steadily. As long as the company sticks to its guns, people will begin to make the choice of whether or not they wish to work in this kind of environment. For those who have already changed their attitudes or are well on the way to doing so, the new environment will become increasingly comfortable; for those whose attitudes remain largely unchanged, the environment will become increasingly unfriendly. In a mobile job market, they will gradually drift away.

The problem comes when too great a proportion of people in key positions retain inappropriate attitudes. A number of companies have found this to be particularly serious at middle-management levels. In some cases major surgery has been necessary to remove many of these people and replace them with fewer, more customer-oriented employees.

Measuring attitudes

To a certain extent, the company embarking on a customer-care programme should have started gathering information on employees' attitudes in its initial researches to define customer needs. It is often useful, however, to assess employee attitudes on a continuing basis, to ensure that top management is aware of progress (or regress) in developing attitudes that support customer care.

The traditional employee attitude survey, whether made by questionnaire or with focus groups, isn't much use in this process. It was designed for a very different objective. Indeed, it can be argued that such surveys do not measure attitudes at all, but employee satisfaction, which is not the same thing. They are also susceptible to outside influences, such as whether there have been rumours of redundancies recently. For the practical purpose of distinguishing between the traditional attitude survey and the kind needed for customer care, we refer to the latter as the attitude audit.

To provide the information management needs for customer-care purposes, an attitude audit has to focus much more closely on issues such as:

- Is the company creating the kind of climate where customer care can flourish?

- What impediments does it create?

- Is it listening closely enough to what employees and customers say?

- Are managers providing the kind of support people need?

- Do people understand the importance of their role in customer care?

Inevitably, this demands much more care in the design and implementation of the research. It may take two or three years before the company has a systematic attitude audit that it is fully happy with and which allows accurate measurement year after year.

Awareness development

Most customer-care programmes kick off publicly with awareness development of some kind. At Booker Foods, for example, some of the customers interviewed in the initial research into perceptions of service were subsequently filmed in their own working environments. Their comments formed the bulk of a twenty-minute video presentation to all employees, illustrating the best and worst aspects of the company's service. An external trainer then led a series of discussions with employees at each location on the theme, 'What shall we do about it?'

Because the employees themselves usually made the suggestion to set up action teams to look at major problems, the degree of commitment at the lowest levels was relatively high. Moreover, the process of attitude change had already begun; by participating in the discussions and catching something of other people's enthusiasm, many whose attitude had been that 'nothing will ever change round here' began to take the lead in making change happen.

Behaviour

Behaviour is the last component of change. It has to be constantly reinforced by attention to structure, systems, standards and attitudes – and by training.

Ideally, all customer-service training should be the result of a need identified by the employees themselves. In other words, it will be much more effective if people ask for it rather than have it forced upon them. That is an additional good reason for separating awareness (part of attitude changing) from training (part of behaviour changing). Of course, people will learn a considerable amount from going through the analysis process that awareness seminars spark off and they may need some training to work out their roles, responsibilities and interfaces. The important thing is to be clear about the sequence of events:

1. Awareness

2. Analysis of training needs

3. Training

If employees are involved in the first and last of these steps, it becomes difficult to justify excluding them from the intervening step. The benefit is that they understand from the beginning the relevance of the skills they are about to acquire. Moreover, the training department has a valuable touchstone against which to test whether or not the particular training is needed.

One of the problems with many packaged approaches is that they lump awareness building and training together, so employees do not have the opportunity to participate in this way. That sends an immediate message – 'We know what's good for you' – and has the inevitable result of reducing employees' sense of ownership. No matter how much the programme may talk about new, more democratic and open ways of management, it is impregnated already with the assumption that management knows best.

Moreover, the packaged approach assumes that the training needs will be uniform across the company. In most cases, that is manifestly not so. By allowing the employees to participate in the setting of training objectives for their team or department, a company can focus rapidly, effectively and selectively on those training areas where the need is greatest. For example, it may be much more valuable in terms of customer service to train people in an accounts department, which deals with numerous queries, in telephone techniques rather than to rush them into seminars on problem-solving.

Performance appraisal

In the discussion on reward systems, we touched briefly on the need to include customer-care measurements in performance appraisal. Every company will want to do this in its own way. However, managers who have been through the process of defining roles, responsibilities and interfaces with all their staff will normally find that they can conduct a much more structured and outcome-oriented discussion during performance appraisals than would normally be the case. They also have a much broader range of sources of information about performance, from both the customers and the other side of the person's various interfaces.

All of this arms the manager and the individual employee with a great deal of information from which to analyse current and future training needs. In particular, it means that training recommendations will be based more on customer-related objectives and less on internal, operational objectives.

5

GETTING A CUSTOMER-CARE PROGRAMME UNDER WAY

Before going too far into the practicalities of setting up a programme, let's review what actually happens in one that has been working for some time. The service-improvement cycle illustrates the process of continuous improvement at the operating level (we'll come to the strategic level later). It starts by raising people's awareness of the need for change. That need is expressed in terms of a mission or as specific goals. Ideally, people at the operating level should be aware of the goals of the organisational layers above them, if only to put their own department's goals in context, but they don't necessarily have to sign on for the grander goals.

Information collection about customer needs cannot always be done by the employees, but management should ensure that they have opportunities for involvement, even if it is only to talk to the people who do gather it. The standards for meeting those needs should then be set wherever possible by the employees themselves, in consultation with their manager. The manager must, none the less, reserve the right to overrule, although he or she should use it only sparingly.

Meeting the new standards will often mean investment in training, in new technology, in new systems and perhaps in new premises. Once made, these changes need regular monitoring to ensure that they have delivered what was intended.

In most cases, some additional tinkering or consolidation will be needed. This provides the opportunity to reward people for their part in making the improvement successful . . . and the cycle begins again.

The service-improvement cycle

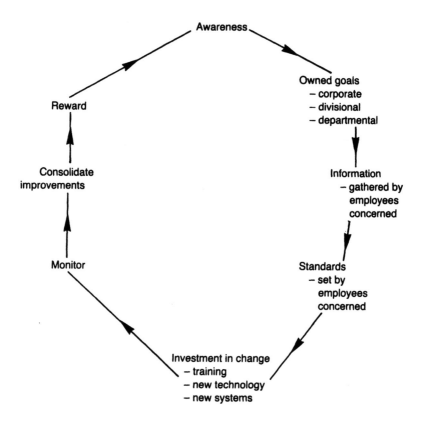

In practice, there will often be several cycles running at one time within a department, each relating to a different goal. Getting to this stage takes time. It will happen only if the customer-care programme is:

- planned in a thorough but flexible manner as part of a clear and widely understood strategy;

- adequately resourced, both in terms of money and top-management time/commitment.

The planning process has to be the result of combining an assessment of customer needs (both current and predicted), the organisation's resources (both current and obtainable) and the potential added value that can be created by using the latter to meet the former. When most companies approach strategic planning, they tend to work from the business they are in, then look for opportunities to meet market needs. A truly customer-oriented company starts from the customers' needs and then examines its potential to fulfil them profitably. All of this sounds pretty obvious and has been said in different ways many times before, yet very few companies take the customer-oriented planning route.

This attitude towards planning at the top has significant implications throughout the organisation. For a start, attitudes have a habit of filtering down. If top management isn't 'thinking customers', it is unreasonable to expect other people in the organisation to do so. Moreover, if structure truly follows strategy, then it will be much more difficult to build a genuine customer-oriented organisation.

So step 1 is: *get the strategy right.*

Of course, strategic planning can take place only with adequate information, so the first stage of getting the strategy right must be an investment in a substantial analysis of the customers and their needs. Once the strategy is clear, the company can start work on a detailed plan of implementation. In particular, it will need to assess the resources available. How much time can top management put in, not just for the launch but on a continuing basis? Has it got the people it needs to meet defined customer needs? How long will it take to train them and how much will it cost? What are the physical changes it will have to make? And so on. Many companies grossly underestimate the resources they will need to make the customer-oriented strategy work, because they do not understand how large a change they are embarking upon. Take time to analyse where and how strongly resistance is likely to occur, how it can be overcome and what that will cost.

So step 2 is: *create a detailed and realistic resources plan.*

Next, top management must kick off an awareness programme. Before it does so, however, the Chief Executive Officer must ensure that at least a majority of his or her team are both fully conversant with what is intended and fully supportive of it. In creating what is effectively a new organisation, he or she should examine the existing team closely. Will they be able to perform well in the new environment? If they can't, they may be a severe drag on the entire project. One large British company, for example, found that initiatives in its customer-care programme were constantly being blocked by the operations director, a powerful number two in the management hierarchy. This person saw the project as dangerous, because it would inevitably expose weaknesses in the operations and he considered that that would be a negative reflection on him. Eventually, after several attempts to change his attitude by persuasion, the chief executive recognised that the only way to make the programme work was to fire the operations director. Just because customer care is about 'being nice to people', it doesn't mean that you can tolerate obstructive behaviour. In any programme that works, there will be tough people decisions to take. The earlier they can be taken, the better. The awareness programme will normally work down the organisation, cascade fashion. Built into it should be a feedback mechanism that gives top management an objective view of internal attitudes and of how people are responding.

So step 3 is: *convince people of the need, starting from the top.*

Once people understand the need, many of them will want to do something about it. Rather than impose formal structures – that takes too long – capture that first flush of enthusiasm by creating the opportunities for them to devise their own initiatives. The idea of forming a small team to look at a customer-service issue will occur to most groups of employees naturally; no need to suggest or impose it, simply support it. Encourage them to go ahead now, while they are still keen, rather than waiting for a training programme to show them how. The initial successes of these teams will provide the fuel for maintaining the momentum of the programme.

So step 4 is: *make use of people's natural creative response.*

From this time on, speed is essential. The longer it takes to achieve visible results, the more people's initial enthusiasm will dissipate. The short-term objective now is to establish the process of changing structures, systems and standards. The most effective method is to work from both ends of the hierarchy. Top management can make some fairly drastic changes by decree – for example, redesigning the sales force from a product structure to make salespeople responsible for selling a range of products in a smaller area. It must also put in the training and other resources needed to support such changes. At the bottom level, employees at the primary customer interface can begin to work with their managers on defining and understanding their roles, responsibilities and interfaces, and identifying immediate changes that can be made within their departments. As changes from the top work down, change from the bottom gradually works up.

So step 5 is: *start making real changes fast.*

Of course, there aren't normally the resources to get everyone involved in making change happen at the beginning. In some companies, for example, middle management and staff departments may be completely overlooked at this stage. These people need to be kept informed about what is going on. The objective is to have them constantly asking, 'When's my turn?' rather than, 'I suppose I'm going to have to waste time on this too, then?' Two main methods can be used here. The first is simply to produce high-quality communications, in newsletter or video form, on a relatively frequent basis, explaining the progress so far. The second is to invite enthusiastic people who have already been through the process to visit other teams and talk about what they have done. In many cases, this results in work teams taking the initiative themselves, saying, 'We are going to do this. Will you give us your support?' Wherever possible, top management should put itself behind such initiatives. Where, for resource or timing reasons, the initiative is impractical, top management should go and explain why itself, to emphasise how seriously it takes the employees and their ideas. It is usually very easy then to divert their enthusiasm to areas of change which are practical and relevant.

So step 6 is: *communicate, communicate.*

And step 7 is: *make sure all initiatives receive the support their instigators deserve.*

Finally, when everyone's job has been recast around customer objectives, when all major systems and standards have been reviewed, there comes the issue of keeping the momentum going. The more thoroughly all the previous steps have been implemented, the more the programme will have a momentum of its own. Training needs will emerge automatically from the discussions at each level, and the resulting training courses will give people more confidence to be ambitious in customer service. As they gain experience, so their confidence will continue to grow.

Yet even programmes as well founded and well integrated into the corporate culture as these may founder if they are not maintained. Top management must therefore make it a priority to know and understand how it is progressing. Employee attitude audits and customer-satisfaction surveys will help. Other basic data such as number and type of complaints and percentage of repeat custom will also provide insights. But these will not explain, other than in the broadest terms, whether the cycle of service improvement is turning faster or slower, either in absolute terms or by comparison with customer needs. There is no substitute for senior managers spending time conducting their own periodic audits of the service-improvement cycle. By doing so they can:

- identify at what point hold-ups tend to occur;

- gain a level of high-quality feedback about customer-service issues not available by any other means;

- assess the kinds of investments that need to be planned for in order to maintain the programme's momentum;

- communicate directly to employees the type and direction of change the company wants to encourage.

So step 8 is: *find out for yourself how the programme is progressing.*

It isn't enough just to attend each training programme, whether as a speaker or an observer. The senior manager has to demonstrate his or her interest and commitment by continually coming back for more. People who expect to file the customer-care programme under 'Completed projects' are selling both themselves and their company short. Indeed, top management's visibility and communications on this issue are needed more strongly than ever at this time. No responsible mother would assume that her child was capable of fending for itself as soon as it moved from breastfeeding to solids. No responsible executive should allow himself or herself to abdicate responsibility for customer care just because the programme has gone through its first phase. Like being a parent, customer care is a twenty-year sentence. Once you recognise and accept that fact, it will continue to be a challenging and enjoyable experience.

Part II
CUSTOMER CARE IN ACTION

6

ANGLIAN WINDOWS

'Double glazing is the butt of many complaints – but not just about the cowboys; some of the biggest offenders are the big boys,' claimed Lyn Faulds-Wood, a presenter of the BBC consumer-affairs programme, *Watchdog*.

Watchdog's consumer advocate team severely criticised Anglian Windows when, on 7 November 1988, their programme featured dissatisfied customer Sally Whiteford of Southsea, near Portsmouth. Whiteford's complaint centred on lengthy delays in installing a Georgian conservatory and the resulting building chaos she had had to endure in her home. In this case the fault was not entirely Anglian's: there were mitigating circumstances, including the kitchen's being refitted by others at the same time. Unfortunately, what the viewing public saw was an Anglian customer's home in a mess. 'We see how double glazing can ruin homes and lives,' said the presenter.

Happily for Anglian, the BBC programme has not done any lasting harm. The company has become the largest manufacturer of replacement windows and doors in Britain, since it overtook its competitor, Everest, early in 1988.

When Anglian launched its customer-care programme in 1986, it was trailing in second place. Since then, however, turnover has increased by about 40 per cent to £150 million, while Everest's turnover has dropped to around £80 million. Anglian management is convinced that good customer service increases sales and improves profitability. The reason is self-evident: word-of-mouth recommendation is one of the principal ways that double-glazing firms attract business. In an industry with such a dubious image, having a reputation for customer care clearly gives an edge. Better customer care also reduces costs as it saves the expense of redoing faulty work.

In the mid-1980s Anglian management knew they needed to look carefully at service standards. Sales were increasing rapidly but, according to Marketing Director John Hart, so were minor complaints. In addition, several members of the management team (some of whom had been with the company for more than twenty years) were worried that they were losing the contact they had once had with customers. They felt it was just as important to provide 'a friendly service as a clinically efficient service'.

To this end Anglian management called in the Industrial Society to conduct an independent appraisal of the company's operations. This, they thought, would provide the best starting-point for getting to the root of the problem. The Industrial Society's report made it clear that, while far from being a disaster, there were several areas of Anglian's customer care that could be improved. Two in particular were turnaround of damaged or incorrect items and morale of the staff who dealt with clients most frequently.

As a result, Anglian has revamped its system for dealing with windows damaged in transit or installation or found to be the wrong size on site; such orders can now be replaced for customers within seven to ten days, whereas before this might have taken four to five weeks. In order to make sure staff encountering clients performed in a consistent and proficient manner, Anglian established formal written standards.

As the report put it: 'Customer care is important for all businesses but when, like Anglian, you are dependent on your reputation and image, customer care is absolutely vital. It's all about getting everybody to take responsibility. It's not just about the product. The actions or behaviour of one person can destroy any amount of goodwill.'

Implementing the Programme

The company sees customer care as a circle, with every employee the customer of another. It starts with the customer of the sales person, the external customer. The sales person is in turn the customer of the surveyor; the surveyor is the customer of the order processing clerk; and so it goes on. The transport department is the factory's customer, and the circle is complete when the external customer becomes the customer of the installation team. What this illustration shows, of course, is that cooperation among all departments is crucial to the overall success of the organisation.

Anglian management chose a high-impact programme, starting at the top and involving everyone in the organisation. As Hart says, 'The Anglian view is that customer care is like water – it does not flow uphill.' Although the Chairman, George Williams, did not have time to become personally involved on a day-to-day basis, he did endorse and monitor the programme – a fact that is well known throughout the company. 'Every director was personally involved. Nobody at Anglian was left in any doubt that excellent customer care was a major objective,' Hart says.

The Marketing Director was given overall responsibility for the programme. Management felt that since the marketing department was responsible for selling the dream to the customer, it should also be responsible for ensuring that the dream materialised. Hart now takes care of customer service in addition to his responsibilities as Marketing Director. Previously, no main-board director was specifically responsible for customers and there was no clear relationship between management and customer service. Now clients will sometimes write directly to Hart to tell him about their complaints and he is ultimately responsible for their satisfaction. On many occasions, Hart will visit a site where a problem has arisen – at a weekend – finding this the best way to establish whether his branch manager or the customer was correct in their assessment of the situation.

A Customer-Care Committee consisting of the board of directors and a number of managers decided on the content of the programme. Then branch managers, sales managers and administration managers attended short residential courses throughout the country, run by the Industrial Society under the aegis of the directors. Managers in turn trained their staff in a cascade process.

Everyone was fully informed as to how Anglian planned to implement its customer-care policy with a selection of films and videos as well as a briefing on the report of the Industrial Society. Staff were also invited to make their contribution through the formation of groups similar to quality circles. From these meetings, the company obtained about 800 suggestions on how it could improve its service to customers. Some suggestions were duplicated and some were impractical, but by and large it was the staff who mapped out the improvement programme. Following up the suggestions and putting them into operation cost Anglian a considerable amount of money, but the result was a great boost in employee morale, particularly in the sales force. As Hart says, 'They knew they could talk about Anglian's superior customer service with complete confidence. It was a very strong selling-point in their eyes.'

Problems Encountered

Some of Anglian's middle managers were less receptive to the programme than others because their salaries were based to a large extent on the profits of their branches. Customer care costs money, which, in the short term, is reflected in branch profitability. 'It was an issue which had to be put across in a very positive fashion,' says Hart. Most managers see it as money well spent, now that turnover has grown considerably and the level of complaints has fallen. As he puts it, 'Those branch managers who offer quality service are secure in their jobs. Those who don't are at risk. Of our forty-six branch managers we have lost three, who failed to meet service standards. And we've found that there is a correlation between good service and profitability, anyway.'

Suppliers were another problem. Says Hart, 'Some suppliers had got into the habit of giving Anglian whatever they felt they could get away with, taking their chances that the shipment would be accepted.' Unfortunately, it was frequently Anglian's customers who found themselves in the role of quality-control inspectors, rejecting defective parts. Research on the nature of complaints received by the company revealed that a very large proportion concerned components that had been purchased rather than items that had been manufactured. For example, the majority of complaints about locks could be traced to substandard products from suppliers.

The difficulty, of course, is that the customer does not differentiate between bought-in and manufactured components. Hart offered an analogy with problems faced by the car industry. If, for example, you buy a Jaguar and the gearbox malfunctions, you are unlikely to say, 'The Borg-Warner gearbox fitted to my Jaguar has broken down.' Your reaction is more likely to be, 'My Jaguar has broken down,' and, by implication, Jaguar is to blame. The same applied to Anglian. If the lock on a patio door failed, the customer was not interested in the fact that it was made by a well-known manufacturer and was reputedly very good. In his or her view, the fault lay with Anglian.

Now all incoming goods are examined by inspectors, who check batches stringently. If they find more than two or three defective items, the whole shipment is rejected. Some suppliers have reacted angrily. Hart says, 'We have had the odd supplier stamping their feet and throwing their rattles in the corner, but at the end of the day we are the customer, and if our customers are entitled to expect good service from us, our viewpoint is we are entitled to expect good service from our suppliers.'

Effects of the Programme

Public recognition of, and reward for, good service are now part of Anglian's systems. Hart took an example from the hotel industry. Photographs of the employee of the month with a bronze plaque underneath – to be found in the foyers of many hotels – so impressed him that he adopted the concept, albeit somewhat less flamboyantly. Installation teams now have personal identity cards, which enable customers to nominate that team for the 'Fitters of the Month Award' if they feel that the fitters have given them an exceptional level of service. (The cards also contain useful information such as the telephone number of the local branch and the name of the person who handles customer inquiries.) Every month around 2,500 teams are nominated. The winners, selected by a draw, enjoy an all-expenses-paid holiday. To encourage participation, the customer who nominated the winning team receives a free weekend in a UK hotel.

Anglian management believes that job satisfaction has increased since the programme began. Hart comments, 'Staff turnover, although never very high, has decreased further. People at Anglian are now convinced they are providing a very good service, and they are enjoying their jobs much more. Nobody enjoys working for an organisation that provides poor service.'

The firm's image has also undergone a facelift. As part of the campaign, Anglian extended its corporate identity and enhanced its appearance right down the line, covering personnel, vehicles and equipment. Fitters now have stylish uniforms, with a choice of overalls or jerseys and trousers in navy blue and an Anglian Windows logo on the back and on a front-pocket badge. Company vehicles have received similar treatment. The Wendy-house image, which has worked so well for Anglian in the past, has been adapted for all new additions to the fleet.

Anglian management monitors the customer-care programme closely. Every month it prepares a report which analyses complaints, dividing them into ten categories:

1. Incorrect delivery time quoted by sales representative
2. Delivery price exceeded the company's quoted estimate
3. Bad workmanship on installation
4. Units not up to standard (including problems with condensation)
5. No response to letters and telephone calls
6. Appointments not kept
7. Delays in completing remedial work
8. Survey errors
9. Cancellations, warranties, requests for service calls
10. General complaints

The figures are presented in a league table and circulated throughout the company. The performance of each branch is illustrated on a bar chart, which enables branch progress to be measured on a continuous basis.

Of course, reducing the level of complaints was one of the prime objectives at the beginning of the customer-care programme, and the statistics give a measure of its success. Notwithstanding Anglian's embarrassment at its problems with Mrs Whiteford being exposed on television, overall complaint levels have dropped by over 70 per cent since the programme was introduced in 1986. Hart points to the example of Anglian customer Roger Patterson, who was so incensed after seeing the *Watchdog* TV programme that he rang the BBC to tell them Anglian just wasn't like that.

The company also looks to the bottom line. It is convinced that improvements in the quality of its service have had a lot to do with its advance to the number-one position in the industry.

According to Hart, after three years of running a customer-care programme, maintaining momentum and guarding against complacency are challenging objectives. Anglian keeps tight control over its monitoring system, regularly appraises staff performance and rewards those who give exceptionally high levels of service.

The Future

As part of its efforts to do even better, Anglian is currently attempting to gain the British Standards Institute award BS5750 for the level of manufacture and service in its factories. It also hopes to establish a system of self-inspection in factories whereby employees on the production line are responsible and accountable for the quality of the work they produce. Most of the factories are introducing a bar-coding system, and the company envisages a time when each worker at every stage in the manufacturing process will put a personal bar code on to each product. Then, if a problem arises from a defective component, its bar code will reveal the history of its manufacture. If the problem is a recurrent one, or if the employee is unwilling or unable to provide the quality of service required, he or she will be replaced.

The Ten Commandments seem to have an affinity with customer care, and Anglian's technical services department has drawn up its own, which it offers to other firms:

1. Provide good communication – it is vital to ensure a positive attitude
2. Know your customers – know who they are
3. Talk to your customers – use names
4. Get involved – define your customers' needs
5. Set yourself standards and resolve to achieve them – always
6. Present yourself well – neatness and confidence inspire the same
7. Check that your remedies to your customers' problems are up to date – their problems might have changed
8. Be flexible – modify your plans to suit the situation
9. Get involved in the customer-care campaign – advise the representatives of things you think should be done
10. Be polite – in person and on the telephone

7

AVIS UK

Avis UK is the market leader in Britain's car-rental industry. The company has a strong tradition of customer care and has always enjoyed the reputation of being the 'friendliest' car-rental service. It has turned that approach into a very successful business, recording profits well in excess of its major competitors.

Avis's customer-care programme began as a two-part study undertaken by a firm of consultants, involving a detailed customer survey followed by a staff survey to look at employee attitudes to delivering the service. The results, for a company with a good reputation for customer care, were salutary. For example, many of the problems highlighted in the survey were not coming through to the complaints department, and about half of the customers who had problems did not tell Avis about them. So, billing and money complaints did come to the complaints department's notice, but unclean cars or car breakdowns were matters that customers tended to keep to themselves.

On the staff side, the consultants identified a so-called 'positive morale problem'. This occurs where employees are highly committed but find that the company's structure frustrates their efforts. What Avis needed was not a customer-care programme in the usual sense but what former training manager Richard Davis calls a 'service leadership programme', aimed at transferring responsibility from head office to the station forecourt.

Implementing the Programme

Avis's first stumbling-block was a classic management problem: responsibility without authority for the frontline customer-service person. As Davis explains, 'If you want people to perform, they have to own their problems. They have to be responsible for them. And they have to be able to do something about them. No amount of training will do anything if, having given staff the skills, we don't give them the authority to do anything.' Management designed the programme to address this problem.

The company did, however, start with two new training programmes, for frontline and head-office personnel, in May 1988. The intensive two-day programme for frontline teams (including station managers) focused on empowering them to deal with customer-service issues and helping them to feel comfortable with the authority this implied. For head-office staff, the sessions concentrated on how best to help the frontline teams and other internal customers.

Both types of training also stressed the difference between customer service and customer satisfaction. Providing service, according to Davis, implies a master–servant relationship and a simple process of reaction to a customer's spoken needs. Providing satisfaction, he says, is more proactive and requires staff to anticipate customers' needs in addition to delivering service efficiently.

In both programmes, trainers explained what the customer-service problems were and what the customers were saying, according to the survey results. They worked on making people more confident about what they would be doing. The initial training was effective in communicating the need to create customer satisfaction. These sessions were followed up with team-building exercises, which focused on finding out where individuals stood within the company and how they could contribute to its success.

During the initial stages of the programme, Avis also looked at the complaints department. Davis comments, 'If customers' complaints are handled well, they become loyal customers. We found that customers with complaints that are dealt with well become more loyal than they would have been if they had never had a complaint.' Management decided to upgrade the complaints department into a strategic department and also turn it into a profit centre, following studies by the Tarp consultancy. A model designed by this consultancy can actually calculate the profit impact of complaint handling.

The upgrading was more in terms of employee status than a physical improvement, says Davis. The company appointed a more senior manager to head the department in summer 1988 and re-evaluated its computer technology. The new manager has made a major effort to cooperate with frontline teams.

But customer dissatisfaction is not just a matter for the complaints department. As Davis explains:

> Many of Avis's complaints are about the vehicles – the availability of a preferred model, mechanical problems or cleanliness, for example. Queuing and delays at stations regularly spark complaints. This sort of niggle can cause a lot of dissatisfaction. We feel stations can turn the customers' perception round at the time. We want our customers to leave us with the magic phrase in their mind: 'I'm glad I rented Avis.'

This is possible only where stations have the tools necessary to solve difficulties as they arise. The real problem in implementing the programme came when they tackled this fundamental issue of 'responsibility without authority'. Davis points out:

> You cannot look at customer care as a programme. There are a lot of companies who just try to train it in. When this occurs it is easy to notice the superficial behaviour. Three months later it has all worn off and they are back where they started. Customer care is not a training issue – it is a process of total-quality management. This involves

altering the management structure, so that decisions are made at the front line and upper management takes on more of a support role. This can cause problems among middle management, however, if they feel responsibility is being taken away from them.

And that is precisely what happened. Middle-management resentment was aggravated by the fact that the training programme was implemented under a rigid time limit. This created a good deal of pressure and left certain areas of the company somewhat unprepared. When frontline staff were told they were responsible for customer satisfaction, middle managers were hit with some staff wanting to make decisions and some panicking because they were not capable of doing so. Not surprisingly, middle managers reacted badly and wondered what the training department was up to. The crisis was overcome in time, but it served to highlight the fact that managers at all levels need time to adjust to new ideas.

Effects of the Programme

Avis has not tried to measure the effect of its 'We Try Harder' programme in terms of revenue. Instead it has used two measures: customer complaints and customer satisfaction. The results have been encouraging. The company measures customer satisfaction by evaluating repurchase intentions. These in turn are measured through questionnaires sent out each month to customers, says Training Manager Kieran Maloney. Davis adds that the information from these questionnaires is sent back to the station manager involved. There are three types of question on the form: those that deal with service attributes, such as how clean the car was and whether it arrived on time; those that deal with the customer's overall satisfaction; and those that deal with whether the customer would rent again from Avis, and the reasons for that decision.

Internal change is necessary if people are to be convinced that the organisation is committed to customer care. In Avis's case, various strategies have been devised. One of these is a recognition of good work in the form of rewards. Avis's ' "We Try Harder" Award' allows customers to acknowledge good service. Another scheme, called 'You Tried Harder for Me', is aimed at commercial customers. Davis comments, 'Avis tries to create as many opportunities as possible for people to be noticed when they do the right thing. This is a very important part of the "We Try Harder" programme.'

Avis also invites staff to make their own suggestions for improving service. 'I believe that our staff have the answers to most of the problems,' Davis says. He explains that much of this side of things is handled by the Core Group, which is made up.

> of middle managers from operations and other departments within the head-office function, who look at Avis's quality of service and seek new ways to improve it. They can act as a think-tank, but they have a degree of responsibility to become an action-tank as well. Since we started the Core Group in November 1987 we've been amazed by how many of the initiatives have come from staff suggestions. The staff survey told us that we weren't very good at listening. The Core Group exists to correct that. We can look at all the ideas that people have. We need people to have regular meetings and ask: 'What can we all do to improve our service?'

One of the biggest advantages is that the organisation has always been very shallow, with only four steps from the front line to UK Managing Director. 'Key issues are dealt with by cross-functional matrix-style meetings,' says Davis, 'and rental locations meet monthly to review progress and standards. Every training event reinforces the strategy. Induction courses, for example, involve a case study where students spend the afternoon as the UK management team.'

Avis still has more to do, however. Organisations do not make fundamental changes overnight. Davis explains:

> We need to devolve even more responsibility to the front line and change the emphasis on central control that we inherited from a traditional multinational company history. A current exercise, for example, has been to convene a task force of station staff to review our service standards to anticipate any changes and developments in the travelling customer. As a trainer I see my main task as the steady involvement and change of the managers in redefining their accountability – *to* their staff, not *for* their staff.

Obstacles to Customer Care

Davis points to three main difficulties faced by the company as it works to improve its standards of service. First, the customers themselves can be aggressive, demanding or intimidating. In the car-rental business customers are generally at their lowest ebb. They are not making a 'glamour' purchase but rather a distress or urgent-need purchase – not something they want so much as need – and Avis picks up all the stress from the customer in this situation. Customers tend to be especially temperamental at airports, having just negotiated their way through the bureaucracy of immigration and customs, with jet lag to boot. This places an enormous demand on customer-contact staff to be helpful and friendly while they are being shouted at. The second difficulty staff face is the responsibility of the job. Avis service staff are responsible for a mobile asset (each car is worth on average £10,000) and must decide whom they can allow to drive it away. They are, after all, responsible for getting the car back. The final obstacle, however, is company administration. 'It is a constant struggle to make internal systems and procedures as customer-friendly as possible,' says Davis.

The Future

Davis concludes:

> Avis has to keep moving towards an ideal. The whole issue of customer care is a process, and Avis has just started this process. In principle, all we have done is rediscover something that Robert Townsend and Colin Marshall created in Avis thirty years ago. Avis was the pre-eminent car-rental service and they provided it very successfully. The essence of the process forward has to be creating and defining a role for every individual in the company and his/her responsibility.

His message to other companies is simple: 'Stop looking to training programmes for answers. If you want quality, you have to look at how your company is structured. If you have this fundamental belief, then everything else should fall into place.'

8

BOOKER FOOD SERVICES

Booker Food Services (BFS) distributes goods to the catering industry, supplying Britain's hotel and restaurant chains, independent caterers, fast-food outlets, schools and hospitals. Part of Booker plc, a major public company, BFS is a young, ambitious firm that has grown through acquisition to become the market leader, with total annual sales in excess of £200 million.

Booker attributes much of its success to 'the implementation of a programme of customer research which identified how Booker Food Services could best meet the stringent needs of today's progressive caterer', to quote from its promotional literature. The research consisted of exhaustive surveys conducted in 1986 with purchasing directors, catering managers and head chefs. It identified five critical elements demanded by customers:

1. Deliveries must be made on time

2. Orders must be fulfilled in every detail

3. Individual requirements must be completely understood and acted upon

4. A multi-temperature, single-drop service (i.e. a single delivery of ambient, chilled and frozen items) must be available

5. Communication between customer and supplier must be complete

In other words, Booker's customers demanded a complete distribution facility. Meeting this need required a major investment in staff, technology, transport and product range, but most of all it meant an absolute 'commitment to service' – a commitment that is now embodied in the company motto, 'Growing through Customer Care'. Putting the motto into practice was the task of Booker's total-quality programme.

Implementing the Programme

John Black, Booker's Managing Director, launched the programme at the firm's 1987 annual conference. The conference was attended not only by Booker employees but also by representatives of companies like British Airways and Rolls-Royce, who had cooperated by letting BFS managers see their customer-care programmes in operation.

'During that particular conference we wanted to show that everyone was behind customer care at Booker, from senior management down,' says Alan Dashwood, BFS's Total-Quality Controller.

The programme began in earnest with a series of training and awareness sessions. A booklet entitled 'Your Part in Booker Food Services' and a video were produced, and discussions on quality – what it meant to the company, how it affected the customer and what the benefits would be – took place. An important message that management aimed to get across was, as Dashwood says, 'that customer care runs right across the company because everyone has a customer – there is the internal customer as well as the external customer'.

BFS has incorporated customer-care training into its induction programme for new recruits. It has also continued the programme through steering groups and project teams, bringing together employees from the various departments in each depot. These groups act to heighten awareness of the need for quality at every stage of day-to-day operations. They have also provided valuable suggestions on how to improve efficiency: for example, by placing small blackboards where goods are out of stock in the warehouse to tell pickers which alternative to use. The groups are also useful for ironing out communication problems because they include members from all departments in a depot. Dashwood notes, 'The scheme has succeeded in creating an awareness among all employees, including staff who are not actually involved in serving the customer directly, that it is the customer who matters.'

Booker's 'Team Leader's Guide' explains how the continuing programme works:

The Total Quality Programme is run by the BFS Total Quality Controller, who will provide support if you find difficulties along the road to customer care. He has the full backing of the Board of Directors, who in turn will be fully involved in the Total Quality Programme. They will be attending meetings to watch the programme's progress and will be speaking at project meetings. Their advice and skills will be used as much as anyone's in securing the success of the Total Quality Programme.

The real work of the programme revolves around the Project Teams. With regular team meetings, supported by newsletters and updates from the Board of Directors, we hope to bring everyone's ideas and worries into the open. Only by telling people our concerns can we solve them. The aim of each team will be to identify a particular problem and propose a solution to it. It will not be a case of looking for trouble at BFS, but a positive exercise in improving the way we all work.

The company also organises regular field days, when head-office staff spend a day at a depot working on a job they do not normally do. The scheme has improved communications between head office and the depots, as well as the head-office workers' understanding of the depots' operations and problems.

Booker's approach to customer service has involved more than just staff training. Investment in new technology is also high on the agenda. As Dashwood explains:

> We have invested in the latest computer technology at a new, central contracts centre in Nottingham. From this, we can offer customers the most up-to-date help in price control, documentation, order processing, statistics and management information. Every depot now has an on-site computer capable of reacting quickly to customer needs and supplying the very latest stock and order control information. This has greatly enhanced Booker's 'in-stock' position and reduced the need for substitutes. Booker's disciplined but flexible approach means we can provide a complete and individual service for all types of customers from national chains to small, independent operations.

Investment in modernising and improving equipment has also paid dividends by enhancing service levels. At a cost of over £6 million Booker has brought in new multi-temperature vehicles that allow a one-drop delivery service, saving administration time for customers and ensuring all products reach their destination at the temperature required.

Early problems

According to Dashwood, Booker's biggest mistake at the outset was with the steering groups. Initially top management encouraged depot managers not to get involved, in the belief that their presence might inhibit staff, but this proved to be the wrong approach. With the managers not fully involved, the steering group tended to operate like workers' committees rather than participating in a joint approach to quality improvement. 'Now the managers are taking a much more active role,' he comments. 'They answer questions as they are raised at meetings and everyone can see better why some things are not working.'

Because of this early problem, the company also decided to attach a director to each steering group. The directors attend as many group meetings as possible in order to demonstrate top-level support for the programme. They then report to the board steering group on their progress with specific projects.

Another problem was a lack of time. Fitting everyone into the awareness sessions and training programmes without upsetting existing customer deadlines was, and remains, difficult.

Effects of the Programme

For a young company made up of a conglomerate of acquisitions, the total-quality programme has 'forged a corporate image and brought everyone to the same standard', says Dashwood. It has also generated a lot of enthusiasm within the company. 'The meetings are well attended and the programme has done much to improve communications between various departments within depots. Everyone's suggestions are discussed in detail, and some long-standing problems have been discussed and sorted out within the groups.'

The customer-care programme also led, in early 1990, to the introduction of a quality-assurance manager. This individual inspects warehouses and keeps abreast of the legislation regarding hygiene with which Booker has to conform. The new Food Safety bill and all its ramifications are high on the agenda.

Finding objective means of evaluating the effects of a

customer-care programme is always a problem. One of Booker's solutions combines an objective measure with a reward system for service excellence. The 'Depot Quality Cup', first awarded in 1989, measures depot performance based on four criteria:

1. The results of a random customer questionnaire

2. The results of an internal, depot survey

3. The in-stock level, and the use of substituted products

4. Improvements in the level of operating costs as a percentage of sales.

Dashwood sends a half-yearly survey to 480 randomly selected customers in all sectors of the business. He also uses regional exhibitions for face-to-face interviews with customers. 'We find that our customers can explain their answers better in person and appreciate the personal contact,' he says.

Another measure used by Booker is a 'Risk Management Competition'. This is run annually and sets criteria for the health and safety aspects of the business.

Suppliers

The customer-care programme has also had an impact on Booker's suppliers. 'If our suppliers cannot provide 100 per cent service, then we will not be able to provide a good service to our customers,' says Dashwood. 'For example, if we have to substitute items because of a supplier's failure to deliver, it reduces our customer satisfaction and service levels.' So Booker has started a 'Supplier/Vendor Rating Project', which monitors the level of service it receives from suppliers. Those who fail to meet its standards are given an opportunity to improve. If that doesn't work, the supplier is dropped.

Complaints

At Booker the majority of complaints are received via the telesales department or the sales representative. Each depot has a standard form and deals with complaints in the same manner: recording details of the problem and making sure that action is taken and followed through. Dashwood relates an example of a complaint from a customer who was receiving incorrect orders each week. The problem was reported to the distribution manager at the depot concerned and the customer was told that orders would be double-checked by the manager before they were released. To back this up further the manager arranged for a sales representative to call on the customer every month to ensure that everything was running smoothly. Reports from that customer indicate that the problem has been solved.

The Future

BFS management has ambitious plans for the future but is under no illusions as to how far it still has to go to fulfil its mission statement to:

> Deliver the right goods
> In the right manner
> At the right time
> Every time!

As Dashwood says, 'Gone are the days of untrained people, unhelpful attitudes, dirty, unrefrigerated trucks, and scruffy outdated warehouses. At Booker we have a basic philosophy: if BFS is to continue to expand its service, it will only succeed by caring for its customers.'

The advice he offers to other companies is that *everyone* must realise they have their own part to play. Customer care has to run right through the company – not just in one department or depot, but through the whole business.

9

BRITISH AIRWAYS

British Airways may not have been the pioneer of customer care in Britain, but there can be no doubt that its 'Putting People First' programme was a trailblazer for many businesses. When asked who they looked to for a role model before setting up their own programmes, practically all of the companies we interviewed mentioned BA.

BA was the offspring of a marriage in 1974 between British European Airways and British Overseas Airways Corporation. The result was one airline with two cultures – a company perceived by its staff as two separate organisations. In 1981 Prime Minister Margaret Thatcher appointed Lord King (then Sir John King) Chairman. His brief was to get the then loss-making company ready for privatisation. Among the changes he made were sweeping cuts in the workforce – from 60,000 to 35,000. But perhaps Lord King's most important decision was to bring in Colin Marshall (now Sir Colin) as Chief Executive in 1983. Marshall spent the best part of that year looking at how the business operated, and decided that a fundamental change in the way the airline functioned was necessary if BA was to survive.

Not surprisingly in a large nationalised company, a bureaucratic style of management reigned. Little was known about BA's customers and operations tended to take priority over customer service. This situation gave rise to minimal service standards of a sort that would be unheard of only a few years later. For example, says Customer-First Manager Justin Pannell: 'We tended to give stodgy, typical airline food. It was good food, but it was not meeting the healthy diet requirements of the contemporary customer.' Another problem was the range of fares on offer; there wasn't anywhere near the choice available today.

This culture was, in many ways, a throwback to the earlier RAF days and a function of BA's nationalised status. In short, BA was operationally driven and, to survive as a privately owned business in the 1980s, it needed to become market-driven.

Marshall felt that the staff could be motivated with rewards, but words like enthusiasm, commitment and responsibility were not part of management vocabulary at the time. 'Putting People First' was launched in 1983 in an effort to change the culture of BA and turn it into a market-oriented company.

Says Pannell:

The point was to get everybody to understand who their customers are and what we have to do to meet their needs. There had to be a change in attitude and culture, so that staff would treat customers as individuals. We're probably only half-way through this process of cultural change, and frankly, I don't know if we'll ever get there because we're not operating in a static environment.

Market research was the first crucial task. As Pannell says, 'There is no point in thinking we have an excellent company when the customer thinks otherwise.' BA targets 150,000 customers a year at airports to find out what they think of various aspects of the BA product: phone calls, travel agents, check-in service, in-flight service, baggage delivery and so on. It conducts a weekly audit of its top twenty stations, which account for 60 per cent of passenger traffic, and an in-flight survey, where random passengers are asked for their views on the service.

The cabin crew now have an initiative called 'Serve to Win

Every Time', in which they talk with passengers aboard the aircraft and later pool their ideas from these conversations at meetings 'on the ground'. Managers join these meetings to share the feedback. 'This gives a snapshot of what is going on in the business,' explains Pannell. 'It's finger-on-the-pulse information.' What BA has learned is that continuous market research, looking at both customers and competitors, is essential to planning and to defining standards of performance.

Implementing the Programme

The first of BA's three customer-care programmes, 'Putting People First', running in effect from November 1983 to June 1985, was originally designed by Time Manager International for Scandinavian Airlines. BA thought the core messages were right, but tailored it to suit its own needs. It added to the programme by asking its directors what they thought the key issues would be in the coming two to three years, and what the staff would need to know. From the beginning, the moving force was top management, starting with the initiative of Chief Executive Colin Marshall. 'Commitment from the top is certainly not lip service,' says Pannell. 'It is total commitment and this cascades through the organisation.'

'Putting People First' had four elements:

1. It looked at how passengers experienced BA: were the systems and services user-friendly? were they operationally designed or designed for the customer?

2. It changed the training systems to add customer needs to the focus on technical competence

3. It created opportunities for frontline staff to improve and develop the service: the customer-first teams were the equivalent of quality circles

4. It set up a major new communications programme, the centrepiece being the two-day training event, 'Putting People First', for the entire staff of 35,000

The ultimate aim was to get people to 'eat, sleep, live the values and demonstrate the values', says Pannell. 'If any of these are missing, the programme will not work. You will spend a lot of money, and waste your money.'

The training for 'Putting People First' delivered three core messages:

1. Staff must own passengers' problems

Says Pannell: 'As a symbolic representation, imagine a member of staff pointing to someone else. For that one finger pointing forward, all the remaining fingers point back to the first person. The moral is that customers don't care whose problem it is; they just want to see it sorted out.'

2. Staff must be actively involved with and committed to the programme

This was achieved primarily through groups called customer-first teams, which were set up on a voluntary basis to identify possible service improvements. Customer-first teams tend to fall into one of three types: (a) ongoing teams, which can have a life cycle of several years, meet every month and have set problems to solve; (b) project teams, involved with one-off projects; (c) cross-functional teams, where staff in different departments with common problems meet either for a particular project or on an on-going basis.

3. The bureaucratic style of management cannot continue

BA recognised that the training would be wasted if a bureaucratic style of management persisted, so its 1,200 managers also received training in the form of a one-week course called 'Managing People First'. The twenty-four participants who attended each course had to begin by giving five assessment forms to their subordinates, five to their peers and one to their boss, all of whom were asked to rate them on their behaviour. As the course unfolded, participants identified what the 'ideal manager' would be like, and then found out how they compared to the ideal.

Importantly, the training was followed by a change in the management pay structure to include performance pay. Managers now receive performance bonuses, 60 per cent by achievement of objectives and 40 per cent based on the behaviour they practised to achieve them.

BA made some mistakes in the early stages. At first it designed 'Putting People First' only for the 27,000 customer-contact staff. However, it soon realised that the training should be extended to everyone in the organisation. Customer care was 'a cultural shift of major proportions', explains Pannell. 'It meant that *all* staff had to change the way they worked. That is why the programmes cannot stop; if they do, people may drift back to their old way of working, which they may still feel more comfortable with.'

Initial reactions among the staff were mixed. A behaviour and life-styles course, designed to help staff feel better about themselves and accept change, triggered accusations of brainwashing and imported American ideas. In fact, the ideas were Scandinavian. According to Pannell, many people were willing to give it a try, but there were also a number of casualties at the beginning. Some staff did leave the airline, albeit with generous severance payments.

Parts of the business were more resistant to change than others, and engineering was one of the most difficult areas. 'Engineering people are not necessarily known for their people skills,' says Pannell. 'It was a total change to their view of the business.'

There were other problems too. 'The message was simple, but it was difficult to get everyone to take it on board. Staff were used to stereotyping customers, and we had to encourage them to treat them like individuals . . . You cannot launch a quality programme until you have the staff attitudes right,' he continues. 'You have to spend a lot of time finding out what makes staff tick and what makes customers tick; combine the two, and then get the parties to understand each other's point of view.'

Two subsequent training programmes evolved from 'Putting People First'. First, there was 'A Day in the Life', which ran from November 1985 to December 1986. It involved ten theme presentations to explain the workings of different divisions within the organisation, such as operations, marketing and computing, and to get staff used to the idea that they were all pulling together. Run entirely by BA staff, it gave people an introduction to the procedures of departments with which they might not normally come into contact.

Then, there was 'To Be the Best', which ran from May 1987 to June 1989. This was effectively the corporate goal. The principle was that if each department was the best it could be, then collectively the business would be 'the best'. Departmental forums encouraged staff to identify strengths and weaknesses within the airline and suggest improvements to help BA surpass the competition on all fronts. These sessions asked individuals to look at one of five airlines representing a threat to BA, and to do a SWOT analysis (identifying the top four 'Strengths, Weaknesses, Opportunities and Threats') for each. The sessions finished with a summary of the other companies and showed how BA measured up to the competition. Trainers then explained that for these five companies, another 175 could be added. As Pannell describes it: 'The purpose was to remind employees that they should not become complacent, because the competition out there is tough.'

Effects of the Programme

Improving customer care has also involved structural changes in the organisation. 'The people who know how to solve problems best are the frontline staff and frontline managers, with guidance and strategy from head office,' Pannell notes. BA's structure has become flatter and broader over time in order to push power as far down the line as possible. It has also reduced management numbers. Although flat organisations can have difficulties with communication across the ranks, BA's decision-making is now much faster. BA sees it as a competitive advantage to have people who can make decisions on the spot while other airline managers have to refer similar problems to head office.

Hiring criteria have changed as well. For customer-contact jobs BA is now looking for people who like to be with people, who work well in a team and who can cope with the rigours of the job. The 'person specification' for cabin crew has been modified to focus on interpersonal rather than formal service skills.

The lower birth rate of the 1970s means that fewer young people are coming on to the job market, so BA is now recruiting staff in an ever more competitive labour market. The glamorous image of the airlines is an advantage, but BA still has to offer its workforce attractive career prospects. The appeal of being part of a successful and prestigious organisation does give BA an edge, Pannell believes.

Increases in job satisfaction are always difficult to judge. However, as he comments:

In 1983 people wanted to know where the company was heading. Now that goal has been defined, more demands have been placed on the staff. Productivity per employee continues to increase; at the same time, people better understand what they are doing and find their work more satisfying. The better the service, the more compliments they receive from customers and the more successful the company becomes. It's a virtuous cycle.

Measuring the effects of the customer-care programmes on the business is just as difficult. With different programmes for different departments and levels of management, including internal awards for staff who excel in customer service, it is impossible to quantify the effect that any one programme has had. Overall, though, Pannell notes that 'if there wasn't a major cultural change, it is arguable whether we'd still be in business'. And BA is growing, both by gaining market share from competitors and by taking advantage of a growing market for air travel. In fact, it is now one of the most profitable airlines in the world.

According to Pannell, it is the people in BA who have enabled it to distinguish itself from other airlines. Some aspects of airline service are easy to match. Says Pannell: 'If BA puts an 8-ounce steak on the menu, everyone else follows suit. But the culture that lies within British Airways is not something that can be copied easily. Customer care cannot be switched on overnight, and this is what we hope will keep us ahead of the competition.'

The Future

As Pannell sees it, the major obstacles to improving customer care are outside BA's control. Increasingly, its biggest problems are with air-traffic control and airport congestion. The company is working hard to improve relations with the British Airport Authority (BAA), its landlord at Heathrow, and is pushing equally hard for a fifth terminal there to improve facilities for customers.

BA was privatised in 1987. Therefore half of its customer-care programmes were carried out while it was still nationalised. One of the major thrusts of future programmes will be the idea of BA as a *business*. In addition to customers and staff, BA now has a new set of people to answer to – the shareholders. With 74 per cent of the staff holding shares, BA can approach staff as co-owners of the business, with obvious benefits. Moving on from its goal 'To Be the Best', the new target is 'To Be the Best and Most Successful Company in the Airline Industry'.

1992 presents an obvious challenge, though it remains to be seen whether an open market in Europe will create fundamental changes for the airlines. 1992 will certainly bring 'Freedom of the Skies', enabling BA to fly to any EC destination, cut fares or double frequency without the bilateral agreements between aviation authorities and airlines that have operated so far.

BA sees the industry becoming increasingly globalised, with airlines continuing to merge into bigger conglomerates. Profitability is the key to survival, but many state-owned airlines are in the same position as BA was in 1981, with little motivation to act efficiently and cost-effectively.

At the end of the day, says Pannell, 'The closer we get to our customers, the more likely we are to get their business, and the more prosperous we will be as an airline.' This is BA's basic marketing strategy, and it is one the company believes will ensure its survival well into the future.

Pannell offers the following advice to other organisations:

1. Find out who your customers are

2. Find out what your customers want from you – what you think is important might not be important to them

3. Get staff involvement and commitment in the process – people must understand and believe in the values of the company, and demonstrate that belief

4. Ensure commitment to customer care comes from the top down.

'If any of these is missing, the programme will not work and you will be throwing away your money,' he says.

10

BRITISH GAS

British Gas has seventeen million customers in a virtual monopoly. Privatised in the late eighties, it embarked on a carefully
researched customer-care campaign to help it grow and develop
over the coming decades. The campaign has proved successful
and thanks to a series of concerted measures, customer perception of this utility has improved.

Robert Evans, who became Chairman in July 1989, was one
of the key players, believing that caring for customers was the
only way forward.

The company jumped into action in October 1989, sending
over 500,000 surveys a day to its customers who were asked to
complete and return them in pre-paid envelopes. The survey,
called 'Banishing Gripes', asked customers a variety of questions on a number of subjects, including installing and repairing appliances, telephone enquiries, meter reading and bill
payment options. But the survey didn't stop there. It also asked
customers to state what irritated them most about British Gas
and to suggest other areas where service might be improved.

Evans, of course, was completely behind the initiative, saying: 'This is a mammoth task, but the results from the survey
will be invaluable. The key to commercial success is providing
service of the highest quality. You can't do better than ask your
customers what they want.'

Over a million customers took up the offer to say what they
thought of their gas providers and, needless to say, their

comments varied. The highest ratings were awarded for reliability of supply, followed by prompt attention to gas leaks and the provision of helpful options on ways to pay the bill. The lower ratings, which were for the disruption caused by laying and repairing gas pipes and dealing with telephone enquiries, indicated areas on which British Gas knew it had to concentrate. Not surprisingly, lower prices were listed as the most important factor which would improve customers' view of the service.

The company used the results to target certain areas for improvement. These included:

- a significant reorganisation of the gas business to enable problems to be sorted out quickly and easily at local level

- the continued introduction of cost-effective new technology to link the mobile workforce with the depots

- an evaluation of new technology for meter reading which could substantially reduce the need for estimated bills

- the further implementation of the major developments that have been made in equipment, techniques and practices to help keep road excavations – and associated disruptions – on the public highway to a minimum.

It didn't respond to demands to lower the price of gas, but one of the concrete results of this huge and costly exercise was a guide entitled 'Commitment to our customers', which ambitiously pledged an efficient all-round service from friendly, courteous and skilled gas people. It also offered an improved complaints handling procedure and fair compensation for customers who are genuinely disadvantaged by broken appointments or by other service faults. Having identified the best practices through the survey, the pledge endeavoured to make them the norm and not the exception, including:

- a warm welcome, personal attention, good service and expert advice from all gas showrooms

- a helpful and friendly approach to all telephone enquiries and correspondence with customers by gas people happy to give customers their names

- a facility which enables customers to contact any gas office within their region for the cost of a local phone call

- morning or afternoon appointments for service work – with fair compensation if appointments are not kept without proper notice

- a top class same-day service, where possible, for essential repairs

- priority attention where the needs are greatest (for example, where elderly, very young or sick people are without heating or cooking facilities)

- more jobs finished on the first visit by service engineers

- better management of gas road-works and better information to local people about any planned mains relaying or repair work.

But this commitment goes even further and gives the company's customer relations managers authority to settle compensation claims of up to £5,000. 'I'm not expecting them to be paying out vast sums of money,' said Evans. 'We are concentrating our efforts on getting the service right because that's what customers want, rather than compensation because it goes wrong.'

This was the first time the company had published standards of service although it had been working to its own internal standards for many years. Mr Evans said he hoped publication of the commitment would help to silence those critics who claimed that service standards would decline in the privatised gas industry.

Disabled and older customers haven't been forgotten in the upheaval. For them, British Gas has introduced a code of practice which gives details of the special services available. The code, called 'Our commitment to older or disabled customers', is designed to increase awareness of existing activities and introduces general improvements. It is available from all gas showrooms, home service departments and local offices. All British Gas employees have been sent a copy so that they are aware of the new arrangements.

One of the most significant developments outlined in the code is the setting up of a register of older or disabled customers, initially in Scotland, and then throughout Britain in autumn 1991. Registration is voluntary, but those customers who wish their special needs to be noted will be invited to contact their local British Gas Region, who will keep them informed and updated on the special services available.

The improvements outlined in the new leaflets 'Advice for Older People' and 'Advice for Disabled People' include:

- an extension of the free gas safety checks scheme

- free gas tap adapters, where possible, for people with hand disabilities or impaired sight

- a telephone call to customers who are blind, giving them details of their gas account every three months

- a free meter move for older or disabled customers whose payment meter is in an awkward position.

Well established safety *do's and don'ts* in the event of gas leak are described in each leaflet.

The third leaflet 'Choosing and Using your gas appliance' lists a number of appliance features which older or disabled customers could find helpful. Energy efficiency is also promoted with a series of energy saving tips.

British Gas has also drawn up a programme to extend and improve its various services for older or disabled customers. The plan has been agreed with the Gas Consumers Council and includes:

- the nomination of at least one member of staff in every gas showroom to deal with all aspects of help and advice for older and disabled customers

- further publicity and promotion of the special services available

- a review of all information displays in showrooms which give advice for elderly and disabled people.

British Gas has worked closely with the organisations who represent the disabled and the elderly to find out what it could do for this special section of its market.

Customers are also encouraged to contact British Gas if they have any difficulty paying for what is often their only source of heating and cooking. In addition, the company publishes a leaflet 'How to get help if you can't pay your gas bill'. This is easy to read and explains exactly what customers should do if they get into genuine difficulty over the payment of a gas bill. In most cases, British Gas will be able to agree a realistic payment arrangement to help worried customers clear the debt.

This service, which was backed up by extensive television and radio advertising, has been one of the company's great success stories. Not only has there been a rise in public perception of the utility as a caring company, but by encouraging people to get in touch and discuss the problem, British Gas has been able to reduce the number of disconnections for debt from 60,000 in 1986 to less than 20,000 in 1989.

The company's reputation for concern for the underprivileged customer was enhanced in 1990 by a teen magazine style publication designed to inform young mothers. 'Girl Talk' is a brightly coloured, educational, but fun magazine published quarterly by British Gas. The magazine gives advice on benefits, child care and, of course, details on British Gas and its product and services. Nurses, midwives and social workers countrywide have welcomed the initiative and demand almost exceeded supply on the first issue.

As part of the move towards better customer service, British Gas underwent what Robert Evans billed 'the most significant organisational change for more than a quarter of a century'. He claimed that the change would enable the company to work more effectively in a changed business environment.

Unlike the former structure, the new organisation is uniform throughout the country. The twelve gas regions remain in place but have been sub-divided into 94 districts to serve the needs of the company's 17 million customers. Each district is responsible for up to 250,000 customers. General managers are appointed to look after the day-to-day requirements of these customers.

The new structure was phased in from May 1990 and will take eighteen months to implement. It aims to focus all company operations on customer needs. As a spokesman explained: 'The general managers will be expected to deliver our commitment to customers and the financial performance required of them. For the first time, customer care is now a specific part of their brief, which is an important step towards improving service.' To help these managers, head office has given them authority to respond speedily to customer needs. They are also responsible for training their staff how to be courteous to customers.

Operations directors have been appointed in the twelve British Gas regions. The operations directors, reporting to regional chairmen, are responsible for a number of general managers.

The new structure allows the organisation to be more flexible and enables developments in research and technology to be introduced more quickly and uniformly.

The hard work and dedication have been worth all the effort, if recent surveys are anything to go by. According to an independent survey conducted in 1990, the reputation of British Gas is at the highest level ever recorded. The study, which has been continuing quarterly since 1977, puts British Gas in sixth position in a table of thirty different businesses. Its previous highest position was seventh which was in June

1987, shortly after privatisation and soon after a well publicised reduction in gas tariffs.

British Gas was the highest placed of the utilities in the table, as well as the best regarded in the energy industry. Electricity has fallen to twenty-second position, while BP has fallen to eighth. Marks and Spencer was top of the league.

The company also fares well in a survey of consumers' views of public services carried out by MORI for the National Consumer Council. According to the survey, 82 per cent of those surveyed were satisfied with their overall gas service. Gas came top of the utilities group and second only to the coach services for customer care, with 67 per cent considering that the company looked after consumers well. The 1989 publication of the Gas Consumers Council recorded a 23 per cent reduction in the number of complaints compared with the previous year.

11

ELANCO QUALICAPS

Elanco Qualicaps is a division of Eli Lilly and Company, a research-based corporation that develops, manufactures and markets pharmaceuticals, medical instruments, diagnostic products and agricultural products around the world. Elanco Qualicaps makes hard gelatin capsules in Europe for major pharmaceutical companies throughout Britain, Europe, the Middle East, Africa and the Indian subcontinent.

During the early 1980s, says Director of Marketing Brian Booth, 'Elanco was operating an inside-looking-out approach to its customers. The company was saying to the customer, "This is what we can do for you," whereas it ought to have been saying, "What do you want from us?" '

This state of affairs was the starting-point for Elanco's customer-care plan. Says Booth: 'We asked ourselves, "Is what we are doing really what our customers want?" We asked customers if Elanco was meeting their current needs and likely to be able to satisfy their future needs.' The responses were not encouraging and suggested that Elanco's attitudes and methods had to change if the company was to remain competitive.

Elanco's customer service has since made a remarkable improvement, and customers have noticed. Says Booth: 'We had a major pharmaceutical company manager in here looking at our operations recently. A few years ago he thought Elanco stood for "Eli Lilly Are Not Customer Oriented". Now, he says, it means "Eli Lilly Are Now Customer-Oriented". That's the degree to which our customers have noticed the change.'

Booth launched the programme with the help of two American consultants. A major issue arising from preliminary discussions was the need for a better understanding of customer needs. The consultants argued that the customers' reasons for buying Elanco products might be quite different from what the company thought, so it was vital to understand how customers perceived the product.

In January 1989 Elanco began to implement its customer-care programme. The consultants had not designed it, believing that it could succeed only if Elanco did that in-house. Instead, their role was to guide the company through.

Implementing the Programme

Elanco began by determining 'What are we doing today?' in terms of service levels, customer needs, delivery times and response to problems or complaints. It then set a target of reducing the gap between current practice and an ideal situation – no complaints, all deliveries on time and so on – by 50 per cent. What is more, this target was to be achieved by 30 June 1989. 'The six-month schedule was tight,' says Booth, 'but it gave us a measurable target.'

The company used customer feedback to measure its service levels, starting with a Customer Performance Report for seventy targeted customers, which was – and continues to be – taken around by the sales force on their visits. Says Booth:

Sales representatives ask customers: 'We are not too sure we know what you want. We talk about price but what else makes you decide to buy, or not buy, from us?' They told us that what they really wanted was a vendor that could make their lives hassle-free. They want to be sure the product performs, that it will be delivered on time and will meet their specifications. Our products are used in their production, so any errors and delays on our part affect their entire operation.

Another priority was to ensure top-management support. 'I addressed the other directors in the UK and throughout Europe to get their support. They passed the information on to their managers so everyone knew what I was doing. Top-management support made it possible,' says Booth.

Staff training also started at the top. Directors set up project teams in the UK and on the Continent. They were to meet regularly to identify the projects needing work, necessary improvements, measurement controls and reporting systems.

Booth organised sessions to explain the concepts to site directors and managers, who in turn decided which employees should be in the project teams. After that, management left the teams to get on with it. Booth comments: 'The management can say this is where we want to be, but they don't know all the details of how they are going to get there. It is better for the staff themselves to say that if this is where we have to be, then this is the best way to do it.'

One of the programme's central elements was to show staff how their behaviour affected the customer's perception of the company. As Booth says:

In a large corporation with many different levels of management and different departments, it is very easy to develop a business style where a piece of paper passes from one department to the next, and staff rarely know what happens to it once it leaves their department. So it is important to explain to each member of staff what happens in each department and to show the effect of, for example, a one-day delay. It may cause a five-day delay in another department, thus reducing customer satisfaction. Everyone had to come to understand the role they played in the company as a whole.

Elanco also called quarterly site meetings to inform staff of the progress made since the last meeting. During the second round of meetings, in spring 1988, managers asked: 'What do you need to make your job easier and more efficient? What isn't working right in your department?' The staff then came up with a list and discussed each issue in small teams led by one of the project team members.

Booth explains what happened next:

> Managers then turned the whole matter around and said to the staff that they as management were not the best people to solve problems; these were best tackled by the people who had to deal with them. Managers asked staff to suggest solutions. Although response was initially poor, people did begin to volunteer after the second request. The change in roles and attitudes has done a lot to boost staff morale and build pride in the company. There is now a noticeboard showing who has helped to solve a problem and what this has meant to the company and the customer.

At site meetings these days, managers find out what progress staff have made in solving problems, rather than the other way round. But this has brought in its wake a new challenge: learning how to set priorities. 'You can finish up with a list of 100 problems,' says Booth. 'Everyone takes assignments and comes back three months later with solutions to perhaps 10 per cent of them. Not one whole problem has been solved. So it is important to find the major issues and give these top priority. Otherwise no achievement is made and people get frustrated.'

Obstacles

Elanco encountered a number of difficulties when implementing its customer-care plan. First, there was resistance from some long-serving employees, whose reactions were: 'Why do I need to know this? Why do I need to start doing this?' As far as they were concerned, they were satisfactorily employed in a successful company.

Says Booth:

> A lot of management and employees are, traditionally, not too interested in what the next guy does. I had to gather everyone in the process, from the initial customer enquiry to the delivery, and walk them through it so each could learn how they impacted upon the rest of the operation. I think people came to understand that their work – and their delays and mistakes – had a knock-on effect through the whole organisation. They began to feel, 'Hey, we do make a contribution and it is recognised', and began to take greater pride in their jobs.

Enthusiasm for the programme grew. 'People began to work as a team,' he comments. 'They started using slogans like "They are us" and "We are them".'

Another difficulty was that top management did not fully understand the importance of staff involvement in all aspects of the business. As a result, in some of the early project teams not all the necessary personnel were present. It took time for management to work out who did which job and what the importance of certain individuals was to particular tasks. They struggled to get the right people in the right teams, and to understand the sensitivity of the staff who were not included.

The next problem was one of communication. In the early stages management tried communicating the results of the programme in the traditional way: director to manager, manager to head of department, and so on down the line. But they soon found that this chain tended to break down as people went on holiday or were off sick. Results were not passing down to the people who had been working on the projects. This system was abandoned in favour of announcements at briefing meetings, information on noticeboards and various other opportunities for all members of staff to get the message. Another obstacle that has yet to be completely overcome, says Booth, is determining just what the customer wants.

The answer you get depends on who you speak to in the company. The production manager, marketing manager and financial manager will all give different answers to the same question. Not until we find out what we are being measured against can we try to deliver what the customer wants. The other challenge is that these measurements keep changing, so every time the sales reps go to the customer, they have to verify that the customer is still using the same set of measurements.

Effects of the Programme

Improvements in efficiency – particularly the time it takes to process customers' orders – is one of the positive effects noted by Booth. But the biggest benefit to date, he says, is that 'we feel more professional internally and have more motivated and understanding staff'. In other words, job satisfaction has increased significantly. 'People are now saying that their jobs are much more interesting. They didn't realise how much of an impact their job had on the business. Our customer-care programme has got rid of the idea that managers wanted employees to leave the thinking and decision-making to management.' Now that staff are involved in problem-solving they realise that management recognise they can be more than 'button pushers'.

Suppliers have also felt the impact of the programme. Elanco's purchasing staff now bring suppliers on site to explain their needs and the criteria they have for assessing suppliers.

Perhaps most important of all, the programme has had a positive effect on the bottom line. Says Booth: 'Profitability has definitely improved. There has been a significant turnaround in the performance of the business unit.'

Elanco began its customer-care plan with targets determined in large part by customers themselves. Those targets for June 1989 were met and the company will continue to use the Customer Performance Report to set its targets and measure its performance.

Though the programme has not been running long, Eli Lilly has been impressed and has extended it to other divisions. 'It has been a very good role model for the corporation,' says Booth. 'We still feel there is a lot to do, as the customers' needs are always changing and the competition is improving as well. But it is good that other divisions have seen the effect on staff morale and professionalism.'

Maintaining the programme is the next challenge, says Booth. If customer care is to become embedded in the culture of the company, if it is not to be seen just as a drive or promotion, the momentum obviously has to be kept up. Elanco has attempted to achieve this in a number of ways:

1. By communicating success and failure, and the impact these have on the customer

2. By continuously raising the targets for customer care, so that people do not become complacent and improvements are always made

3. By giving recognition to staff when targets are reached

4. By demonstrating to staff the effects their efforts have on the business's sales and profits.

The Future

Booth said that he could not forecast Elanco's future moves since 'they depend on customer needs . . . But everything has to be improved. We have to be flexible with both staff and customers'. He advises other firms not to assume either that customers see you in the way you think they do or 'that all your staff have the same objectives. It is surprising how often managers assume that their staff know what the prime objectives are and that everyone is moving in the same direction. This may not be the case. Before launching a customer-care programme, find out first what your customers and staff really think'.

12

FOUR SQUARE

Four Square, a pioneer in providing drinks out of home, is no stranger to quality customer service.

As one of the Mars companies in Europe, the concept of quality – one of the five principles of the Mars organisation – has been ingrained in Four Square's business from the start.

Founded in the mid-1950s as a natural extension to the Mars confectionery business, the Basingstoke-based Four Square enjoys international success in the industry. The company's regional depots and distribution, sales and customer service centres are located throughout the UK, France and Germany and it sells to the rest of Europe through its trade partners.

The company's vending machines and drinks products – KLIX In Cup and FLAVIA Freshbrew Drinks Systems – are supplied to people in industrial, commercial, health and leisure sectors throughout Europe. Klix in particular won Four Square the Queen's Award to Industry for Export as far back as 1981. In 1987, Four Square became the first vending and the second food company to receive accreditation to British Standard 5750, and not long after to European Standard ISO 9000.

Then, in 1989, Four Square implemented a customer-care initiative designed to highlight the importance of quality customer service.

Why would a successful company dedicated to the design,

manufacture and marketing of vending and drinks systems need to be so concerned about customer service? Says personnel manager George Oakham: 'The overall quality of Four Square's service – from fast response to customer calls to courteous servicemen – was pretty good. But there is a big step between pretty good and excellent.'

To make that big step possible, the company moved customer care to the top of the management agenda two years ago at a time when it was looking to improve the non-material quality of its products. 'A vending machine is only acceptable to the customer when it consistently produces quality goods on demand. Four Square provides a service to both the client who buys equipment and the consumer who buys the drinks,' says Oakham.

Six months later, although there were no indications from customers of any serious problems, the Four Square management team agreed to implement a formal customer-care programme. A budget was approved and Oakham, responsible for organisational development, together with Ken Hawkins, the quality manager, took responsibility for championing the cause of customer service.

The first step in the programme, in order to quantify and audit its success, was to canvass associates' opinions through an attitude survey. (Mars companies call their employees 'associates' in order to describe the direct part each associate plays in the success of the company.) The survey asked all associates for their thoughts on customer service and their views on what they believed the customer needed.

Associates reported that internal communications and inter-departmental co-operation could be stronger and problem solving could be more effective. All associates felt they had even more to contribute. In terms of customer service itself, associates were generally unclear about what standards of customer service were required. The further back in the chain from sales to production the associates worked, the less they focused on the customer.

The company's analysis of this feedback suggested that a

high quality training event was needed to launch a long-term customer-care programme. They examined packaged programmes and found that a large percentage of the information had already been taught in other courses to a significant number of Four Square associates at all levels. Eventually, Four Square agreed with a consulting firm to produce a tailored training programme.

The resulting two-day conferences, which were known as 'Putting Customers First', were held in the UK, France and Germany in the appropriate local language. All Four Square associates from every department at every level attended. Said the managing director in his introduction to the course: 'Our mission is to become a leading supplier of branded hot and cold drinks to the out-of-home market. Our competitive advantage will be founded on products offering a unique combination of quality, convenience and hygiene delivered with outstanding customer service.'

To meet such a target, Four Square associates were challenged to develop their personal qualities. In a series of syndicate groups they discussed goals, relationships, stress, non-verbal communication, assertiveness and positive attitudes with their colleagues, and related these topics to customer service.

'On the afternoon of the second day,' reports Ken Hawkins, 'a representative of each syndicate addressed the group as a whole. Most had never spoken in public before, but they spoke from the heart and in their own words about relevant company issues. The effect of these speeches was invaluable: communications opened up between departments, floors, and functions and we all participated in eye-opening discussions with associates we would not normally have the opportunity of listening to.' Oakham agrees: 'The programme highlighted the level of care we were already providing to customers outside the company, but the main benefit has been to focus our attention on the customers each associate has inside Four Square,' he says.

Four Square had recognised from the start that there were

chains of customers stretching from marketing through R&D, production and sales to the actual consumer who ultimately puts money in the machine. Although some associates have no direct contact with the external customer, their attitudes to internal customers – whether service people, sales associates or engineers – can have a beneficial effect on the quality of service received by the external customer.

To keep communications open and to continue the momentum of frank discussions from the 'Putting Customers First' programme, Four Square encourages the formation of customer focus groups. Comprised of volunteers from the same department or work group, the focus groups look at what the customers want. They also address collectively cross-group problems.

'The process for internal communication was always there and it is a core Mars belief that it should be there,' says Hawkins, 'but there was no catalyst.' The customer focus groups, by dealing with those many little problems encountered by associates in everyday work, enable associates to become involved in the decision-making process. This approach enables customer-care processes to follow the same devolved path as other operational aspects of Four Square's business, with decisions being made by the people most directly concerned with any particular challenge. Familiarity with the situation and a fresh approach enable associates to come up with working solutions.

One customer focus group in particular has been quick to use these new internal lines of communication. Five volunteers from the machine factory gathered together to form a quality focus group and highlighted eleven activities as opportunities for improvement in their work environment. They identified spares supply as being the most important issue in terms of putting customers first.

Focus group member Genni Imbert explains the problem that faced the group: 'Supplying sub-assemblies as spares to the Field Technical department, and to customers, was clearly a big problem for the business. Because sub-assemblies were all made on the main production line, and the assembly of complete machines always took priority, spares were being treated as a lower priority. Our objective was to supply a service to the Spares Department that enabled same-day despatch of all production sub-assemblies and fulfilled the daily build requirements of spares.'

The group decided the best answer to the problem was to separate spares production from the main production line. Says Genni: 'We proposed an aftercare service, which really put customers first by ensuring rapid supply of spares for the repair of any machine breakdown.' Although Four Square already offers service packages that guarantee their products for up to 13 years, the company wanted additional support on those rare occasions when a machine does break down.

The group obtained the list of required sub-assemblies, identified a suitable space in the factory and defined equipment needs. Focus group member Mark Whittlesey found the lines of communication opened by the 'Putting Customers First' programme an invaluable asset throughout the project. 'We were fairly scared at first about talking to so many managers, but we were soon able to communicate happily with all levels of associates from different departments,' comments Whittlesey.

The Aftercare Centre is now staffed full-time by Genni. When a customer orders a replacement part for a machine, she is able to send one out almost immediately. 'The customer who requires spares for a machine no longer takes second place to the customer who requires an entire machine,' she affirms. Whittlesey adds: 'The Putting Customers First programme brought home the importance of quality in customer service. With a personal interest in the service of spare parts, we feel closer to the external customer and more valuable as associates of Four Square.'

States Hawkins: 'Since the opening of the Aftercare Centre, the standard of service for spare parts has been fabulous. The customers have actually written in, praising promptness and quality. With such a positive attitude to quality from one end of the customer chain to the other, the external customers – both the client and the consumer – are sure to benefit.'

But how does Four Square measure such benefits? Each year, for the past five years, a random sample of Four Square's customers have replied to a Customer Satisfaction Monitor and rated its service in a wide range of areas. In 1985, 42 per cent of customers rated the overall service of Four Square as very or extremely good. By 1989, this figure had risen to 82 per cent. Since the 'Putting Customers First' programme was implemented, the company has published, internally, a monthly customer service report, which rates the company's service in ten specific areas, including speed of repairs, driver courtesy and accuracy of invoices. The results of this market research indicate that Four Square's customers are increasingly satisfied with the service they are receiving.

The 'Putting Customers First' programme also did much to improve inter-departmental co-operation and understanding of the service function. Associates at Four Square now express confidence in their own abilities to solve problems and they communicate regularly with neighbouring departments. And customer service remains a high, and often discussed, priority with all associates.

'The benefits of the Putting Customers First programme are difficult to pinpoint,' concludes Hawkins, 'but some specific examples are beginning to surface. The Aftercare success is the most visible indication so far, but there are many others. Associates take care to answer the phones quickly, even if that means moving the phones closer to their work space, and other focus groups are beginning to tackle some very challenging problems. I believe the customer will ultimately benefit from improved work practices, increased attention to small details, and more efficient use of time.'

Distribution administrator Stewart Scott is one associate who believes wholeheartedly in the benefits of 'Putting Customers First'. He says: 'The course was an eye-opener. By listening to other associates express their views, I realised I was half the cause of my own problems.'

Before the programme, sorting the paperwork for a particular range of equipment took Scott seven hours to complete. He brought the problem up in a focus group meeting, and various options were discussed. 'In the end,' says Scott, 'it turned out that some of the paperwork was unnecessary – no one had thought to question this before. A lot of figure work was eliminated and a part of my job that used to take seven hours now takes two.'

Scott reports a substantial increase in job satisfaction, as he is now able to spend more time on customer needs – internal or external. 'Problems like mine are now recognised and solved before they affect the customer. With improvements in internal procedures, the chain of customers is encouraged to communicate with each other, allowing associates to spend more time on adding value to customer care rather than just sorting out problems.'

One problem with actually measuring the benefits of training is that it can lead to over-management of customer-facing associates. Four Square believes all associates are responsible for customer care, and they should have full discretion to deal with problems.

Oakham says: 'It is the very passion of involvement that has brought the concept of customer care to life in our organisation. If we were to measure our associates' progress too closely, the flame would die and morale would fade. The associates need to keep the independence and level of responsibility that they've developed so quickly after the Putting Customers First programme'.

However, long-term success in customer care does not depend solely on one training course. Customer care must be a part of the company's wallpaper. In order to continue the quest for quality customer care in the long-term, Four Square has followed up its training with many reminders of customer service – posters, pens and cards are widely distributed to all associates. Since the beginning of the programme annual appraisals for every associate include mandatory customer service objectives as the number one priority. The associate is given a card as a result of the appraisal to remind him or her of what he or she has pledged to do for customer service in the coming year. Current developments include new recruitment and appraisal measurement criteria designed to highlight an associate's orientation toward quality customer service.

Explains Hawkins: 'The reminders serve to keep our customer service goals alive.'

13

KWIK-FIT HOLDINGS

Kwik-Fit's Tom Farmer gained fame as the man who brought customer care to the car-repair industry. Well aware that very few industries had a worse reputation for customer care, Farmer was intent on distancing Kwik-Fit from this negative public perception.

The company had grown from humble beginnings in 1971 to become the market leader in the UK and the largest independent in Europe. Tom Farmer, its founder and now the Chairman, already appreciated what was later expressed in these words: 'The basic philosophy of an organisation has far more to do with its achievements than do technological or economic resources, organisational structure, innovation or timing.'

Kwik-Fit's Philosophy

Kwik-Fit's philosophy lay in the mission statement that Farmer published in 1972:

At Kwik-Fit the most important person is the customer and it must be the aim of us all to give 100 per cent customer satisfaction 100 per cent of the time. Our continued success depends on the loyalty of our customers. We are committed to a policy of offering them the best value for money with a fast, courteous and professional service. We offer the highest-quality products and guarantees. We at Kwik-Fit recognise that our people are our most valuable asset. The manager and fitters at our centres are the all-important contact with the customers and they are the key to the success of the Kwik-Fit Group.

Tom Farmer had thus anticipated what Peters and Waterman later wrote in their seminal book, *The Pursuit of Excellence*:

> Excellent companies are continually responding to changes in their environment; they insist on top quality; they fawn on their customers; they listen to their employees and treat them as adults. In fact, companies with outstanding quality reputations make a conscious effort to get employees involved – at all levels of the organisation.

Kwik-Fit's 3,000 staff now serve over 3.5 million motorists annually with a wide variety of replacement automotive parts, repairs and services. Caring for customers manifests itself in every area of the company through the firm's seven core elements of service: convenience, quality of work, value for money, good service, monitoring, communication and caring.

Convenience

Customers who want a service or a repair done do not want to travel further than they need to to get it. Kwik-Fit has invested in an increased range of services and repairs through diversification and the number of new sites, so more and more customers can take advantage of the convenience factor. Today there are over 620 centres located close to where people live, work and shop, all offering a pleasant, comfortable and clean ambience, as befits today's more affluent and aware customer.

Ambience is not just an empty buzz word. To the fast-fit operator it means the conditions which make a person feel comfortable and welcome – clean, modern building with clean toilets, heating for when it's cold outside, and a comfortable place to sit while you're waiting.

Quality of work

Once a car has been brought in for service or repair, the customer expects that to be the end of the problems. What is offered must be backed up by guarantees, and since the retailer is liable for the work done for his or her customer, Kwik-Fit offers guarantees which are additional to manufacturers' guarantees.

But good workmanship needs good training. Each member of staff must know exactly what they have to do, do it right and do it right first time. Surveys in the United States have shown that manufacturing companies waste an average of 25 per cent of their resources correcting mistakes, while for service companies the average is higher still at 30 per cent.

An important part of doing it right is involving the customer. The Kwik-Fit customer is shown what will be done before the job is started and what has been done once it is finished. Gradually the mystique of the garage workshop is eliminated and customers appreciate that the company is being honest with them.

Kwik-Fit's first training school was opened in 1982 at Newcastle-under-Lyme and the second in Edinburgh in 1987. There are now training schools in France and Holland and a fifth, outside London, is projected. Additionally, there is a business school in each of the five Kwik-Fit divisions. Every employee is scheduled for training in all the areas that have an impact on their career paths and their relations with customers: sales, administration, technical training and management development.

The cost of training is now over £2 million a year – over £10 a week for every member of staff. This outlay is considered to be an excellent investment.

Value for money

Kwik-Fit, like any other good retailer, sets out to offer value for money – a hassle-free operation in which customers get what they pay for. Research has shown that arguments over the size of the bill are the most regular problems for garages. Yet there is no reason why a customer should not be aware of what expert car repairs and maintenance are going to cost. Menu pricing is an answer to this problem. Kwik-Fit has been computerised for many years and offers a quotation which is always the same as the final bill.

Good service

The definition of marketing, according to the Chartered Institute of Marketing, is: 'The management process responsible for identifying, anticipating and satisfying customers' requirements profitably.' A much more common understanding of the retailer's role is this restatement: 'providing the right goods, at the right quality, at the right time, in the right place, at the right price'. Kwik-Fit has added another dimension: 'coupled with the right service'.

Service is not something that depends solely on the person who deals with the customer. It involves everybody, from the telephonist, who is often the first point of contact with the customer, right up to the commercial director or the chairman. And it certainly includes the customer liaison department, or whoever is on the receiving end of an inquiry or a complaint. The company encourages all employees to understand that 'service' includes everyone on the pay roll.

Monitoring

No company can be satisfied that it is giving the right service unless that service is monitored. Kwik-Fit has conducted research through Gallup and this confirms that what customers are concerned with is convenience, price, guarantees, the quality of workmanship and staff attitudes. The most frequent response to the question, 'What makes you decide which specialist fitting centre to use?' is, 'I've used them before and been satisfied.' The second most common response is 'convenience', followed by 'personal recommendation'.

Kwik-Fit also receives through customer-reply cards 150,000 reports annually on the quality of operation. Every report of dissatisfaction is followed up, often in person, not only to ensure that the customer is satisfied but also to find and solve the root problem where necessary.

Kwik-Fit managers practise MBWA (Management By Walking About). They learn what goes on at the sharp end by looking and listening.

Communication

Communication between customers and the company must be mirrored by communication between the company and its staff. Kwik-Fit abhors the NETMA attitude (Nobody Ever Tells Me Anything), for NETMA businesses are bad businesses. The ones that practise effective communication are the good and successful ones. Kwik-Fit produces a weekly news-sheet, a battery of newsletters, promotions, incentives and posters aimed at people in the business and, where appropriate, at customers.

Employees are entitled to know how successful Kwik-Fit is, because they not only draw a salary from the company, they are also, in many cases, shareholders, thanks to a free shares scheme. A financial report to staff is an annual event.

Kwik-Fit's communications programme was summed up in

a *Management Today* feature a few years ago. It read: 'Possibly no workforce in Britain is subject to more sustained corporate hype than Kwik-Fit fitters. Notices emphasising shared commitment are everywhere; they would put a Russian factory to shame . . .'

Tom Farmer suspects that the key to total commercial operating success lies in management's ability to communicate. But, unfortunately, there are far too many managers in British industry who still believe that their status depends on knowing things that the workforce doesn't. This is just not so at Kwik-Fit. It has deliberately set out to shorten lines of communication and to train managers to understand that their function is to support the people on the shop floor. Even Kwik-Fit's modern head office in Edinburgh is called the Support Office.

Caring

Kwik-Fit has set out to create and implement a policy of caring. Customers must come first, for if there are no customers, there is no business. But staff will care for the customer only when they know the employer cares for them. Such caring can be demonstrated in a variety of ways at Kwik-Fit: through a progressive ,vage structure that recognises the individual's contribution to the company's growth and success; and through career paths which offer individuals the chance to develop their full potential, all the way from fitter to divisional director.

Kwik-Fit's unique profit-sharing scheme – entitled 'Partners in Progress' – is the foundation of its retail outlet operation. Those staff who demonstrate that they have the skills and drive necessary to develop their own, and their staff's, future are appointed 'Kwik-Fit Master Managers', responsible for the running of a centre. In addition to their salary, they receive a share of their centre's profits.

Groups of three centres come under a Kwik-Fit Partner. As well as being responsible for their own 'base' centre, they are also responsible for the operations, standards of customer service and profitability of the other two. A Kwik-Fit Partner's remuneration includes a share of the profits from all three centres.

All field staff participate in profit-sharing so that everyone in operating centres has a powerful incentive to reduce costs and maximise sales and profits. They are among the best paid in the industry.

The Future

The company's continued growth, even in the face of adverse economic conditions, proves that the policy of caring for customers and staff is working. Customers obviously accept the two Kwik-Fit propositions. First, you can't get better than a Kwik-Fit fitter (and not only customers; in 1988 Kwik-Fit was awarded the British Midland Diamond Service Award for Promise Fulfilment). Second, without acceptance of the promise of 100 per cent customer satisfaction, Kwik-Fit could never have launched Centaur, its own-brand components, so successfully. These have achieved in excess of a 40 per cent market penetration in less than three years. All are approved by the Automobile Association, as indeed are the operating centres themselves.

For Farmer himself, there is no shortage of industry recognition. In 1989 he received the Scottish Free Enterprise Award from Aims of Industry and was named as Scotland's Top Businessman by the Variety Club of Great Britain. Already in 1990 he has won recognition from the British Institute of Management, which has invited him to become a Companion – its highest award – while the Chartered Institute of Marketing has named him as Scotland's Marketing Man for 1990. He is the first to proclaim that these awards are recognition of the team that he leads, but perhaps he is proudest of what *Management Today* said of him in 1986: 'It cannot be said of many businessmen that they transformed the face of an industry.' Nothing would please Tom Farmer more than to find others in the industry following his example of caring for people.

14

MARKS AND SPENCER

Marks and Spencer might be forgiven for being just a bit complacent. This monumental institution radiates stability and self-confidence, and for good reason: M & S accounts for 16 per cent of Britain's clothing sales – the largest slice of the market by far. For years M & S has been able to count on its good name for quality, value and, not least, service.

Although the firm had had many customer-care drives over the years, it launched a major initiative in 1988. Why? Because complacency is dangerous. Even though M & S's own service standards had not deteriorated, other companies were catching up. The basic aim of the initiative was to increase the firm's lead on its rivals in the area of customer service and to reinforce the importance of the service principle once again.

The first thing M & S did was to set up a Quality Service Group, composed of employees from a variety of backgrounds within the company, including a main-board director, a number of executives and a few managers. Outside consultants were brought in to work with the group. Its first task was to carry out an audit of opinions among both customers and staff through personal interviews and questionnaires. Of approximately 5,000 staff interviewed, the majority, about 3,000, worked in the head office.

According to Mike Shaw, Store Recruitment Manager and former Coordinator of the Quality Service Group, 'Our staff are generally more critical than our customers. They tend to be hypercritical of themselves. The business is not one that has been brought up on a lot of praise, and they feel this is what has made the company great. They are constantly trying to improve.'

From the survey the group highlighted areas where it needed to concentrate, including, says Shaw, 'the need to give good service to both external and internal customers'.

M & S also looked outside the company when setting up the programme, examining well-publicised customer-care programmes in such organisations as British Airways, Jaguar and Scandinavian Airlines.

Implementing the Programme

The entire organisation – head office and stores – was involved in the new programme. The chief executive launched it at a major meeting attended by all executives and divisional directors in August 1988. 'Without support from the very top, the programme didn't stand a chance of success,' says Shaw. 'We have consistently used this link with top management.' All the store managers were also involved through regional meetings.

The essential elements of the programme consisted of a video, training sessions and a workbook. 'It was important that the programme was not too low key for highly intelligent staff, nor should it be pitched too high, so that the average frontline staff miss the point,' says Shaw. To maintain a consistent approach, managers met first and had the programme explained to them. They, in turn, held meetings for their staff. The company brought in extra video playback units to enable managers to hold the programme with small groups in their own offices.

The slogan for this first stage, completed within a couple of months, was 'Making the Best Better'. The programme delivered a common message across the company: identify internal and external customers and work on what they want from you and what you want from them. 'Right through the chain, the processes are all going to be different, but the messages are the same,' says Shaw.

One of the first developments was the appointment of three technical managers to work permanently with suppliers on total-quality-management concepts, in order to implement TQM practices throughout the supply chain.

With food manufacturers, M & S has always insisted on very high hygiene standards and inspects suppliers' factories to see that these standards are being adhered to. If food arrives at the depot at the wrong temperature, it is rejected. Agreements with manufacturers allow M & S to reject merchandise that doesn't reach specifications. Through TQM it hopes to continue improvements at the supply end so that such rejections – which cost the company in terms of increased administration and lost sales – decline even further.

M & S has occasionally been unable to find suppliers to meet its high standards. For example, when it tried to set up a distribution network for furniture, it could not find a UK company to provide a national home-delivery service to the standards and volumes required. So it set up its own.

Vehicles delivering furniture are equipped with cellular phones so that, in case of any delay, the driver can contact the customer. (The company has found that customers mind less if deliveries are late if they are informed of the fact.) Delivery staff even take a doormat with them to wipe their feet on before entering a house. Before handling upholstery, which is covered by plastic sheets that attract dust, they put on gloves to avoid making finger marks. This is just one example of M & S's determination 'to be better than everyone else,' says Shaw.

M & S has also made improvements in meeting consumer demand. Says Shaw:

Customers are very colour-conscious and, in certain areas such as knitwear or leisure wear, we were not able to react quickly enough to demand. The lead time for increasing the supply of a particular garment was about twelve weeks. By then the opportunity to increase sales would be lost. So, together with our suppliers, we now use piece-dying techniques when we see which colour is in demand. This increases our ability to respond to customer needs with a new lead time of around three weeks. We are reacting better to the needs of the market, thereby increasing customer satisfaction.

M & S also made a number of store and company changes to meet customers needs better. In the initial survey customers consistently requested fitting-rooms. Although they recognised that the stores had an excellent exchange and refund policy, shoppers still wanted the opportunity to try goods on in the store before they purchased. This put the company in a dilemma, as most stores were already short of sales space. At the same time, however, they didn't want to deter people from buying. A trial in twelve stores was undertaken, resulting in an excellent public response and a drop in the refund rate. Fitting-rooms have now been installed in all but the smallest stores.

Effects of the Programme

Quality service has now been incorporated into the initial training period for all new staff. M & S has always included the idea of good service in its induction training, but with the new programme this is now accorded a higher priority. A video giving new recruits practical examples of how they should and shouldn't react in different situations is one part of the exercise.

Existing staff appear to be enthusiastic about the programme. M & S receives many letters from appreciative customers, thanking it for the level of service, and Shaw believes that this must have a beneficial effect on employees' job satisfaction. In addition, staff come up with suggestions for improving services, many of which are acted upon. Store managers are free to implement suggestions for their own store to improve service locally.

'Collect by Car' is one example of just such an innovation born out of customer needs. The service, which allows customers to collect their shopping from the loading bay at the back of the store, has proved very popular – not to mention profitable for the company.

M & S also transformed its information-technology systems very quickly over a two-year period. 'It was up to the managers to see that people released from the stockroom and the office through the use of this technology were made available to customers. Five years ago many staff would have been involved in counting everything and have been too busy to help customers,' says Shaw.

Overall, however, M & S found it difficult to measure the effects of the programme in profit terms. Instead, in order to establish the standard it measures queuing times and the time taken to reply to a letter or to answer the phone. In this way managers can see if their efforts are having a quantifiable effect on service levels. By setting guidelines and targets for store managers, M & S is trying to create objective measures for performance.

The Future

When asked about the company's future plans, Shaw replied that it was a matter of 'making sure that the initiative is kept alive at all costs'. Having got the programme up and running, the biggest problem has been to maintain its momentum. The company conceived the quality-service programme not as a drive or campaign, but as an on-going initiative. It was particularly important for the cynics who 'had heard it all before' to be convinced that quality service was part of the culture of the company. Maintaining the interest of staff, particularly at head office, has been something of a struggle.

As Shaw explains:

In the past Marks and Spencer has flipped from area to area; different managers focused on different issues. The chairman might decide that service is not good enough, so we'll have a service drive. Someone might decide that there is too much paperwork, so we will have a good-housekeeping campaign. All of these drives are good in their own right in that they bring you up to scratch in a certain area. But it's like spinning plates – you get one going, and then you start on another, and before it stops you go back to the first plate and give it another spin. But what often happens is that the plates at the back fall off and no one notices until someone goes round the back in a few years' time and sees that all the plates have fallen off. Now Marks and Spencer are trying to learn from their past mistakes by making this not just another campaign but a fundamental part of the culture of the business.

Apart from the cautionary tale, Shaw was unwilling to give any advice. 'This is what gives Marks and Spencer the competitive edge, especially our training video. We don't want to give too many of our trade secrets away.'

15

MECCA LEISURE

What do you do when the staff just want to have fun? Recruiting 4,500 inexperienced seasonal staff every year with the grand incentive of just over £2 per hour does not bode well for customer-care initiatives. Yet Mecca Leisure Holidays, in an effort to give its holiday centres and hotels a competitive edge, has come up with an award-winning customer-care programme that has become the envy of the British leisure industry.

Mecca Leisure Holidays personnel director Ewan Park understands his staff and knows that to get the customer-care message across, it has got to be fun. And fun it is: Mecca is probably the only company in the world to use cabarets and treasure hunts in its training programme.

It has been well received by the experts as well: in 1990 the programme, called 'Quality Through People', won a National Training Award for Mecca Leisure's subsidiary Warner Holidays, and a similar programme at the sister company Shearings Hotels received a national training commendation.

'Quality Through People' was first developed in Warner Holidays, which has operated about ten holiday centres since 1933. But it was not until 1987 that it went into the holiday business in earnest, acquiring another seventeen centres from the Ladbroke Group. The following year the acquisitive Mecca bought the leisure firm Pleasurama – adding thirty-two holiday hotels and the largest coach fleet in Europe to its stable. In 1990 the Mecca Leisure group was itself acquired by the Rank Corporation.

The formation of Mecca's new holiday division after the Ladbroke acquisition brought with it a new board and a far greater investment in holiday centres. 'It was the right time to re-brand and re-launch all the holiday centres under the Warner name,' says Park.

A good time, too, to improve the quality of the holiday centres and, perhaps, finally lay to rest the ghost of *Hi de Hi*. Holiday centres (Park shudders at the word 'camp') are still saddled with the image of the down-market, post-war holiday camps immortalised by such television shows as *Hi de Hi*. Park is not a fan of such TV memories. 'That was forty years ago,' he protests. 'Retail was pretty pathetic after the war, too, but people don't go on about that.'

The late eighties were also a time of changing tastes in the holiday market. Increasingly sophisticated consumers had tried, and tired of, foreign package holidays and were returning to British holidays with a much clearer idea of what they wanted – and of what was available. Those were the people Warner particularly wanted to attract. A 1988 customer survey showed that satisfaction was high among existing customers: about 85 per cent liked both the product and the staff.

'But still we needed an edge,' says Park.'We wanted to attract new and different customers – those who wanted higher quality holidays and were willing to pay for them. That edge comes in large part from staff, but in the early days I don't think staff – or even managers – realised how central they were to our offerings. When I asked staff what they thought our product was, most saw it in a tangible way, describing it as the swimming pool, the accommodation or the catering. But it's not. What we are offering is a good time and it's the staff who make that happen. So if we could improve staff performance, we could improve the whole product,' he adds.

A customer-care programme was, therefore, essential in meeting two objectives: to smooth organisational seams after the Ladbroke merger and to build the edge Warner needed to move up-market.

But, clearly, an off-the-shelf programme would not do for

Warner's unique, seasonal staff development needs. 'We attract an incredible variety of people. Our seasonal staff includes students and lawyers, lads from Liverpool and PhD candidates,' says Park. All told, these fun-seekers make up 500 year-round staff and approximately 4,500 seasonal employees each year. About half are new to the industry each year and, for many, it is their first job. Another third have worked with Warner in the past, while the rest have had some experience at other holiday centres.

Park, together with John Harrison who was then Warner's management development and training manager, ran a standard programme for the 1988 season while designing a customised approach that, avers Park, 'we knew would work for Mecca Leisure Holidays'. The programme, called 'Quality Through People', was, according to Park, inspired more by conversations with line managers, staff and customers, and Park and Harrison's own experience in the leisure industry, than by the work of other companies or popular customer-care 'bibles' of the time. 'I don't believe in taking a theoretical model and squeezing it to fit a company's operations,' Park says. He does, however, admire the Disney World programme, called 'Traditions', particularly 'the idea that you can hook people on ideas and principles far better than you can with instructions'.

Training

Because so many of Warner's staff are inexperienced, Park and his team chose to design the training programme with 'the lowest common denominator in mind. We aimed at someone who has never been trained, and who's nervous at taking on a new – possibly a first – job, and tried to give them everything they would need to succeed'.

The course instructors, for the most part managers or supervisors, are also well catered for. After following a management development programme teaching them how to run the staff training programme, the managers receive a thoroughly scripted and crib-noted training kit. 'The programme material is designed so non-professional trainers can get the messages across,' points out Park.

The programme, extending over an evening and three full days, gives the staff an introduction to customer care like no other, starting with, of all things, a Customer Care Cabaret organised by the centre's entertainment team.

'Their first taste of training includes games, quizzes and sing-alongs,' says Park. 'We even buy them a drink – one drink, that is. We want a relaxed atmosphere, but we don't want to overdo it.'

Trainees settle down to watch the entertainment team – called Team Stars – perform sketches based on the television classics of British customer abuse drawn from the likes of *Allo Allo*, *Fawlty Towers* and *Hi de Hi*, all with customer-care messages incorporated. The evening culminates with all the staff on stage singing 'Consider yourself at home', from the musical *Oliver!*.

'It appears riotous, but it is well programmed,' asserts Park. 'The cabaret acts as an introduction to customer care and it is also a chance for team building, as the seasonal employees get to mix with the year-round staff. Most importantly, for a first evening, it helps people feel relaxed and at home.'

The following day the 'nuts and bolts' training programme begins with the 'Warner Walkabout'. Park explains: 'Rather than hit them with a barrage of facts and figures, we do a treasure hunt style exercise. New recruits go round the site and find answers to questions along the lines of "What five facilities does the entertainment complex offer?". This way they gather the information they need, but would never remember from a lecture.'

The next module, on health, safety, fire and hygiene, is where attention could well lag. 'This section includes some very serious messages, but the communication is still light and breezy to retain interest,' comments Park.

Although customer-care concepts run right through the training programme, the video *That's Entertainment* is there to hammer the message home. Featuring a tough Glaswegian character from a fringe Channel Four programme, the video represents a highly unusual approach: it is almost a parody of customer-care concepts. 'We went that route because we are, after all, aiming at a group of cynical eighteen to twenty-two year olds. Whatever we do, we can't be patronising. It is a light, entertaining, video, but it gets them to think about customers and to assume responsibility for their enjoyment,' he adds.

After the video come the workbooks. These are interactive, thought-provoking and, through a punchy cartoon format, put across customer-care attitudes and skills. Then, says Park, 'we have to make a waitress out of someone who's never carried a tray – all the smiling and eye contact in the world won't make up for a sub-standard service'.

Warner has raised training in mundane domestic skills to lofty technical detail. The company, through consultation with managers, supervisors and staff, has developed standards for every job from chambermaid to dishwasher.

'We now have a way of running the business, right down to a step-by-step checklist for laying a breakfast table or serving tea,' says Park. The list invariably concludes with: how do I know when I've done it right and how will it affect customers?

It was John Harrison who persisted with his suggestion that the company give these standards and checklists to staff members in a filofax. A filofax? 'I was sceptical at first,' admits Park. 'I thought staff would see it as a yuppy idea from management, but when I saw a burly 6'2" chef from Yarmouth carrying his filofax proudly under his arm I knew it would work.' In all, Warner gave away 6,000 filofaxs to staff. 'I was afraid they might bin them, but they respected the gesture and found them useful,' says Park.

The standards themselves should prove even more useful. They are so detailed, and the job skills training so comprehensive, that Warner has been able to link them to City and Guilds qualifications. After completing their training and passing an examination, staff in a variety of jobs, including kitchen, housekeeping and reception, can now gain the relevant, nationally recognised qualification.

'This gives added value to our employment and is part of our goal to be recognised as the premier employer in the holiday business,' says Park. This laudable ambition is not, entirely, altruistic. A good working environment is central to Warner's customer-care – and hence marketing – mission. 'We couldn't stop at a straight training based approach because it wasn't powerful enough,' explains Park. 'If other aspects of the organisation, such as the treatment of staff or the attitude of management, don't support customer-care concepts, the training will not stick.'

So the Warner team concentrated on tackling other long-standing obstacles to customer care and employee motivation, including pay, accommodation and recruitment. Of the first of these obstacles Park says: 'Staff research showed that low pay wasn't an issue in itself because seasonal staff were motivated by a wide range of factors. All we really had to do was ensure that wages weren't an insult, and that extra effort was rewarded.' As a result, Warner was among the first in the industry to introduce a training-based pay scale. Hourly wages increase by about five per cent after staff have completed the training programme.

As for accommodation, Park admits that some of it used to be 'appalling'. Warner has since invested heavily in improved staff accommodation and has made it a significant part of the company mission. 'The Managing Director himself now insists on inspecting all staff facilities every time he visits a site,' says Park.

Much of the success of this motivation programme hinges on recruiting the right staff in the first place. 'In the past, the company hired 40 per cent of staff without even an interview,' says Park. 'Competitors did it too, but just because everybody does it doesn't make it right.' Perhaps as a result of this *laissez faire* approach, Warner, like other holiday firms, suffered from very high staff turnover. Park, however, refused to accept it as inevitable: 'It is far to easy to institutionalise turnover, but you can avoid it by planning recruitment more carefully,' he affirms. Recruitment is now planned centrally and involves such initiatives as recruitment fairs and a new brochure emphasising the fun aspects of working at Warner.

'It really is fun working at our holiday centres, and we chose to make the most of it,' says Park. 'After all, it is the main attraction for staff. The brochures used to take a rather shame-faced approach, along the lines of "come and work hard and be underpaid at Warner's". They are now much more upbeat, and look less formal and intimidating – we even designed them specifically to fit into a jeans pocket.'

Warner also challenged holiday industry traditions by recognising the departmental heads as the business bedrock they were. Dining room supervisors, housekeepers and other team leaders are now employed on a year-round basis and have been given more managerial involvement. 'These people are absolutely critical to our business. We can't very well expect to employ someone in May and have them running teams within a week, nor can we allow our early season holiday-makers to be guinea pigs,' observes Park. 'For all staff, these changes have made the difference between having a great time and doing a great job. They are always going to party, but now they take more professional pride in their work as well,' he adds.

And the price tag? 'At about £250,000 spread over the first two seasons, I think the programme represents terrific value for money – especially as the impact will last much longer,' says Park.

So will the impact on customers. Comparisons of customer satisfaction surveys year by year show improvements in all areas where training was done. Re-bookings, surely a key indicator, are also up markedly.

'Staff turnover has dropped dramatically, and, for the first time in memory, we had no recruitment problems at all this year. And, because we are able to train staff so much quicker, productivity at the holiday centres has already increased,' adds Park.

The Future

Park describes Warner's overriding goal as 'increasing the quality of our products and attracting customers who want that kind of value for money.' – And, of course, attracting the best of Britain's fun-loving resort workers.

16

MERCURY COMMUNICATIONS

Mercury Communications has been described as the telecommunications David to British Telecom's Goliath – and not without good reason. When Mercury began operations in 1982, it faced the giant British Telecom, a government-backed monopoly with assets of more than £10 billion. Mercury did not enter the battle entirely empty-handed, however. It had the backing of its parent group, Cable and Wireless, which invested £650 million in the fledgling company. In four years that investment began to pay off and in the first half of 1988 Mercury Communications turned an £11 million loss for the same period the previous year into a £4 million profit.

Marketing Director Peter Moulson describes Mercury's business: 'We enable people to talk to one another. People now expect instantaneous communication. As long as the system works when they want it to, people don't care how complicated it is. The business has to be invisible.' The company has grown so rapidly that up-to-date figures are difficult to come by, but Mercury's network covers much of the UK, from the south coast to Scotland, from Wales to the East Midlands. By 1989 seventy-five towns and cities were part of the network and Mercury had nearly 10 per cent of the market in the City of London, including all five clearing banks, all of the City's trading markets and institutions and the twenty leading US banks operating in Britain.

Mercury has also moved swiftly overseas. It started handling calls between the US and UK in 1986 and within three years accounted for 9 per cent of all calls to the US, around 11 per cent of calls to Japan and about 4 per cent of calls to the Continent. The company is expanding rapidly in what will soon be the single European market, for it is the only all-digital network in Europe. As Moulson says, 'One shudders to think how large Mercury will be by 1992. We will be a major telecommunications operation on the European scene.' However, he adds:

We did not have a God-given right to succeed. We have succeeded on our own merits through faith, foresight and the efforts of our staff. Mercury is big, profitable and growing fast. The challenge is to sustain this to become an even bigger company with flair, flexibility and imagination, without losing sensitivity to what our customers want.

Quality customer service is now central to Mercury's philosophy, but this has not always been the case. 'Customer service has been neglected in the past,' says Moulson, 'but Mercury has changed that.' Market research by Octagon Services shortly after Mercury began operations revealed that customers did not perceive Mercury's service to be significantly better than British Telecom's. The young company clearly still had some way to go. In the mid-1980s Mercury's top management fused the existing quality-management and customer-service programmes into one new programme: quality customer service. Personnel Director Fiona Colquhoun comments: 'Quality customer service is about team effort, and everyone, whatever their role in the company, has a contribution to make to its success.' Certainly, in a company with an average of 150 new employees each month, it is crucial for newcomers to adopt its culture and understand the competitive issues facing the organisation.

Implementing the Programme

Training for the quality-customer-service programme took the form of a series of workshops, entitled 'The Mercury Way', attended by all employees. These were designed more as awareness-raising activities than training sessions and aimed to give everyone a better understanding of the importance of customer service. Participants were encouraged to look at Mercury in its competitive, commercial context and discover how teamwork could make excellence in customer service a reality. The workshops also introduced the idea of the internal customer: every Mercury employee has a customer and every customer – internal or external – deserves the best efforts of every member of staff.

Mercury believes in training from the top down. 'Unless customer service is practised at the top of the organisation, it is never going to be practised anywhere,' says Colquhoun. For example, when consultants were commissioned to run a series of three-day workshops on quality management, the first participants were the management teams.

Mercury has also built quality awareness into its induction courses for general, technical and sales staff. This training emphasises three points:

1. There is no such thing as good or bad quality; a product either satisfies customer requirements or fails to do so

2. The most effective way to meet customer requirements is to do everything properly the first time

3. Everyone is responsible for the quality of his or her own work; nobody should rely on someone else to judge good or bad work

The training has had an impact on staff, but, says Colquhoun: 'There is still a lot more to be done in this area. The one-day events raised the awareness of the staff, but more training will be needed to increase their skills. We want them to feel confident their performance matches the image Mercury is promoting.'

During the early stages of the quality-customer-service programme Mercury did encounter some resistance. For example, some managers, especially those with a technical background, found the concepts of customer service hard to understand. 'While everybody became aware that the quality-customer-service programme was a major part of Mercury's strategy, some people took it very much to heart and put it into practice, while others failed to grasp it completely,' says Colquhoun.

Effective communication also presented a challenge. 'Sometimes people can see a major obstacle to the provision of excellent customer service, but they do not know if anything is being done about it,' explains Colquhoun. 'The company is trying to overcome this by providing feedback and publicising the results of the programme. If employees are affected by a problem, they feel happier about it if they know someone is trying to solve it.'

Effects of the Programme

To find out what employees thought of the quality-customer-service programme, Mercury conducted internal surveys. Colquhoun says the programme has generated a lot of enthusiasm among staff. She believes attitude surveys are probably the only way to measure job satisfaction.

Surveys might have their built-in biases, but if the same questions are used every time, it should be possible to identify trends. One might not be able to state with complete confidence that 75 per cent of the workforce are happy, but it should be possible to say that the workforce is happier or unhappier than they were the previous year. The same applies to customer satisfaction.

Mercury is about to launch a recognition and award scheme to recognise employees who have demonstrated excellence in customer service. The prizes for winners will include a chance to go parachuting, hang-gliding or canoeing. As Colquhoun comments wryly, 'We hope that the winner sees it as a prize, not a punishment.'

Mercury made a considerable investment in its customer-service programme, but this has paid off in terms of cost savings. A measurement technique, called the cost of quality reporting, relates the programme's costs to the firm's operating costs. In 1989 about 85 per cent of the programme's costs were covered by reductions in operating expenses.

When asked about the obstacles facing Mercury in its effort to provide excellent customer service, Colquhoun said:

> Mercury engineers would doubtless say time and resource constraints are the major obstacles. They do not always have the time to respond to customers in a textbook fashion, or build up relationships with customers, as they are under pressure to perform their tasks as quickly as possible. This can increase their chances of making mistakes and puts the reliability of their workmanship and service quality at risk.

The Future

In such a rapidly growing organisation, customer service is a continuous process. Says Colquhoun:

> There has to be perpetual reinforcement of the goals. Otherwise as the company grows, it gradually loses its focus. I would like it to be seen as part of the culture of Mercury that as soon as employees join the company, they recognise that looking after the customer is priority number one. People need to be selected on the basis of

whether they are prepared to adopt Mercury's values in this respect. This issue needs to be given a higher weighting in the recruitment and selection process of a customer-oriented organisation.

Colquhoun looks for strong identification with the customer on the part of Mercury employees. She gives the example of one engineer who, on his way to work, saw a customer having difficulty operating one of Mercury's telephone boxes. He stopped to show the prospective customer how to operate the equipment. 'Those are the moments of truth for a company,' she says.

Moulson believes that Mercury's regional structure will help keep it responsive to customers. 'Customer demands differ throughout the country,' he says. 'We want to preserve manageable units within the company and establish a regional identity.'

Colquhoun has firm ideas about the level of customer service she expects Mercury to provide. She recounts the tale of a man who lost his American Express card in Iraq. When he telephoned the company, the receptionist stayed on the line until the problem had been solved and funds transferred to him. The conversation lasted for about fourteen hours. 'That is the culture I want to develop here,' she says.

Mercury saw dramatic change in 1990, with a new chief executive, Peter Van Cuylenburg, and the beginnings of a new corporate culture.

The company has taken its quality-customer-service programme a major step forward with the introduction of total-quality-culture concepts (TQC) throughout the organisation.

Total-Quality-Customer-Service Manager John Dawson took on his new position in September 1989 with a brief to implement a total-quality-culture programme at Mercury. 'We are changing the entire culture of the firm. It's an exciting prospect, although we are now only in the early stages. We expect the whole process to take three to four years to complete, as we need that time to get everybody through the training programmes,' he says.

As Dawson explains, the new total-quality culture involves a shift in emphasis towards the three basic tenets of total-quality management:

1. An increased focus on the importance of the internal customer – meaning, says Dawson, 'We treat everyone we deal with inside the organisation as customers'

2. A flattening of the hierarchy to devolve decision-making power down to the front line – as Dawson says, 'Ultimately, we want all problem-solving to be done by the people who have the problems so that not only does the problem get resolved, but also the process is changed to ensure the problem never recurs, and we continually improve the service we provide our customers. We aim to meet 100 per cent of our customers' requirements'

3. The idea of managers as supportive coaches, rather than managers in the traditional sense

'We expect this new way of working to reduce costs through a reduction in wasted effort and inefficiencies. But it is more than a money-saving system, it's a complete cultural change, for now and for ever,' Dawson concludes.

17

RANK XEROX

During the 1960s and early 1970s, when the Xerox Corporation held the patent for photocopying, it enjoyed the luxury of a monopoly position as the only supplier of plain-paper copiers. It took advantage of its stranglehold on the market and became, as it were, a law unto itself. All good things come to an end, however, and for Rank Xerox nemesis appeared when its patents ran out in the mid-1970s.

Japanese firms then entered the market and, offered a choice for the first time, customers started to desert Xerox. Xerox's sales volume and revenue declined, customer complaints increased and, says Customer-Satisfaction Programme Manager Ross Ivy, the firm was losing its traditional service focus. 'We know now and we knew then that customer loyalty comes from consistent and stable service,' he says. 'But when we came out of a protected monopoly position into a highly competitive market we reacted by indiscriminately cutting costs. We even started to cut the service force, but we recognised the mistake of that.'

Something had to be done. In 1981 the Director of Rank Xerox's customer-service division appointed three managers (Ivy was one of them) to investigate what had gone wrong. Why was Rank Xerox receiving so many customer complaints? Why was it inundated with queries about its administration? Why was it losing customers? Why were staff increasingly disenchanted? What was wrong with the way the company worked?

The four-month investigation revealed that the company's problems were basically structural. Like many large organisations, Rank Xerox was burdened with an enormous bureaucracy and an organisational structure that kept functions strictly separate. Communication between departments was non-existent and customers faced a complicated web of communications. First, the sales department dealt with the customer until the contract was signed. Questions, however, could be answered only by the administration department. After installation, the service department took over. Sales, administration and customer-service staff knew nothing about each other's departments, so for the customer, it must have been like dealing with three separate organisations.

Ivy experienced at first hand the problems this system created. Visiting a customer in 1975, he was waiting in reception with a number of other people. When the receptionist called out, 'Rank Xerox', two people responded. Ivy did not know the other person and he did not know Ivy, but they were both working in the same branch. Ivy was part of the customer-service department and the other man represented the sales department.

Xerox's structure meant that there was little reason for the two departments to work together. 'At the time, it wasn't that much of a concern to us if the customer saw twelve people,' says Ivy, continuing:

> It was not a good state of affairs. There were around 5,000 people in Rank Xerox in those days. While it is excusable for 5,000 people not to know one another, it is not excusable for the twenty people who look after one account not to know that there are nineteen other people looking after the same account and not to get to know who they are, and what their account responsibilities are.

These three managers talked to staff and customers to find

out what they did well, what they did badly and what people wanted to do well but couldn't. Top management's first response to their investigation results was to appoint customer-care managers and staff responsible for developing interdepartmental relationships and ensuring cross-functional collaboration.

Ultimately, however, this move proved inadequate. During 1983 and 1984, Rank Xerox expanded the initiative through its 'Leadership through Quality' programme. Originally started by an American consulting firm, 'Leadership through Quality' was among the first quality programmes to recognise customer-care issues and use total-quality management concepts. Ivy describes the programme as 'a set of tools to help us work more efficiently'.

Implementing the Programme

A major push of the 'Leadership through Quality' programme was to coordinate the mission, goals and plans of the firm's various functional departments. The teamwork concept was promoted throughout the organisation via a series of training courses. These were run at an hotel, away from the usual business environment, to encourage participation on a collective basis rather than having managers and their subordinates taking part in a business game. This paved the way for the introduction of the internal customer concept.

A major part of this programme was the development of key-account management and the appointment of key-account managers to look after Rank Xerox (UK)'s largest customers, including the government.

Early problems included some resistance from members of the sales force. 'The company took steps to stop practices which boosted the sales force's commissions at the expense of the long-term relationship with the customer. Some sales people felt this restricted their activities,' says Ivy.

The service division already had a customer-care section but, as Ivy says, 'true customer service started with the development of key-account management, so that Rank Xerox could devise a tailor-made support strategy for each customer'.

The company's salespeople were taken through an account-management graduation programme to help them understand better both customer needs and the operational difficulties within the organisation. Says Ivy, 'The sales force was trained to identify the customers' long-term objectives and endeavour to help them achieve them through integrated Xerox solutions.'

Ivy says the key-account system is now reaping benefits: 'In many cases Rank Xerox has all but eliminated the competition, and become the preferred supplier.'

The manufacturing division quickly embraced the 'Leadership through Quality' programme and, according to Ivy, 'The goal of fault-free production was attained very quickly.' A just-in-time manufacturing system, installed in the late 1980s, further improved efficiency, halving manufacturing costs over a few years.

A central distribution warehouse in Holland supplies all of Europe, but, as Ivy points out, 'The system depends on having a very good relationship with suppliers. We have to be able to trust them to deliver quality products exactly on schedule.'

Getting suppliers to meet Rank Xerox's new standards did present some problems. The company even offered at one stage to provide the services of consultants to help suppliers meet Xerox's quality specifications. 'We did not want to sever any bonds,' says Ivy. Nevertheless, suppliers who could not manufacture to the new standards were dropped in favour of those who could.

In 1987 Rank Xerox completed a full-scale programme which analysed the responsibilities of everyone in the organisation. Its purpose was to enable employees to understand their roles in detail and how those roles related to the functioning of the company as a whole. The organisation can work effectively only when individual departments serve each other effectively and treat other departments in the company as they would external customers and suppliers.

Effects of the Programme

Hiring criteria have changed as a result of the programme and the interview process reflects this. The company now gives a higher weighting to personality tests and interviewers spend more time with candidates discussing customer-care issues. The aim is to select those applicants capable of delivering the highest levels of customer service. However, as Ivy says, 'Customer service skills are not the beginning and the end of the story.' A balance has to be struck between candidates with a proven track record and those with excellent interpersonal skills.'

Performance assessment and reward systems have undergone a change as well. The performance of each team and each team member is now assessed half-yearly by the manager and each team appraises aspects of the performance of its manager in turn. All managers must record the steps they plan to take to improve their relationship and performance with their teams should that be necessary.

In 1988 Rank Xerox was among the first to introduce a scheme linking management pay to customer loyalty and satisfaction. In its first year of operation the scheme affected the top 135 managers at the international headquarters in Marlow, Buckinghamshire, and in the European operating companies. Now, says Ivy, 'All UK managers and service engineers have an element of customer loyalty and satisfaction taken into account in their pay and bonus schemes and in their performance appraisals as well.'

Customer loyalty is assessed by internal measurement of the number of customer products discontinued or returned, while satisfaction is assessed by an independent survey of up to 500 customers. Respondents are asked whether they are happy with Rank Xerox's products and services, whether they would buy from the company again and whether they would recommend Xerox products to others.

The company sets targets for customer loyalty and satisfaction in each operating company, with the current target set at 90 per cent. If the ratings are above target, annual salary reviews can be increased by up to 4 per cent, and decreased if they fall below target. In 1988 the target was exceeded, giving an average extra pay increase of 2.5 per cent for the group.

Said John Pearce, Manager for International Personnel Planning, 'The scheme is having a positive impact on motivation and the way employees identify with the business.'

Rank Xerox also carries out quarterly customer-satisfaction surveys separate from the pay-related survey. These look at the extent to which the company's performance matches the customers' expectations. They also compare customers' perceptions of Rank Xerox with the customers' perceptions of competitors, through annual competitive surveys. In 1982, when the firm first started these surveys, Rank Xerox often came low down the table. Since implementing the 'Leadership through Quality' programme, it has moved to the top three.

Over the last three years, the company has increased its market share by 4 per cent. 'Bearing in mind that Rank Xerox has been operating in a static market, that has been no mean achievement,' says Ivy. Since the increases in revenue have outstripped the increases in costs, profit margins have improved as well. And, says Ivy, 'A correlation has been established between profit and a high score in customer satisfaction surveys.'

Obstacles

Scarce resources are a major obstacle to providing excellent customer care, according to Ivy. 'In the initial stages in particular, setting up a customer-care programme is a very expensive operation. Currently we are investing a large amount of money in a number of programmes, but there are never enough resources to go around, and the programmes which best facilitate the fulfilment of our long-term business objectives have to be supported preferentially.'

He notes, though, that the most awkward obstacle has been changing the culture of the organisation.

It is human nature to like to do things the way they have always been done. Change is disturbing. People tend to like the simplicity of the bureaucratic culture. It is easy to relate to one's boss and subordinates in a unitary chain of command, with tasks transmitted downwards and reports sent upwards. Each department worries only about its own problems and there are none of the difficulties associated with coordinating the activities of different functions. The development of cross-functional processes and teamwork, essential for Rank Xerox to provide the highest levels of customer service, has been one of the most difficult tasks to accomplish.

Part of the solution was the development of integrated-account management, which allows key-account managers access to service and administration data and enables them to obtain the complete status and history of an account. Relationships with customers have improved, as each can now deal with their key contacts instead of myriad disconnected people. The company is working to improve things further by developing sophisticated management information systems to ease the transfer of information.

The Future

Rank Xerox has invested huge sums of money in the development of information systems. These will be the bedrock of its drive through the 1990s. During this time, through integrated work processes, Rank Xerox intends to prove its international capabilities to provide customers with products and services second to none.

Rank Xerox has gained British Standards Institute Certification for its after-sales service. This is an external image and set of standards to live up to, and is further motivation to be the best.

Ivy says: 'Employee satisfaction is a vital element to the achievement of customer satisfaction and Rank Xerox is concentrating a lot of management time and effort to develop conditions, skills and career structures in such a way that they become totally recognisable and supportive to the achievement of our mission, goals and plans.'

Rank Xerox plans to make changes to its customer surveys, which Ivy says lack focus.

'We have used a blunderbuss approach, carrying out a large survey and collating the results. In future, we plan to focus the surveys on the specific needs of each customer. We will agree the content of the survey and respondents in advance with the customer and review it regularly with them. This will enable us to obtain a clear picture of the requirements of specific customers and potentially from that a good idea of the requirements of the whole market. We are on a plateau with regard to market share at the moment, and are developing major initiatives to propel us forwards.'

Finally, Ivy advises other firms to have key measures correlated to the level of customer-service commitment as an integral part of their corporate strategy. Alarm bells should ring when those key measures fall outside a critical zone. Every industry has its own parameters and within Rank Xerox, for instance, one key measure is response time.

There is a correlation between response times and customer perception of service quality. In fact, by keeping a close control of our response times, we can detect as soon as they have gone out of acceptable limits. We can even tell if one of the customer-satisfaction surveys is going to be poor before the results have been calculated, because we know that if the key parameters indicate a drop in performance, it will be reflected in the survey results. Every company should be able to do that, whether it be a supermarket chain like Littlewoods or an industrial-equipment manufacturer like JCB.

18

ROYAL BANK OF SCOTLAND

The Royal Bank of Scotland embarked on its customer-care programme with the aim of gaining competitive advantage over its high-street rivals, but it did not start from a position of long-term decline in service standards. On the contrary, a 1988 survey by the magazine *What to Buy for Business* indicated that, compared with its four main competitors, the Royal Bank was perceived by consumers to be well ahead in efficiency, helpfulness and charge levels. The survey also collated the results into overall ratings by turnover of the businesses surveyed and again the Royal Bank came top in two of the three categories ('£1–£5 million' and 'Over £5 million').

Despite this enviable standing, the bank recognised that simply providing quality customer service was not enough to gain a significant advantage. After all, it was not the only bank to invest in customer care. In its view, the customer must perceive that the company is trying harder than anyone else. As Robert Crawford, Coordinator of Service Circles, says: 'The public remember the extremes of service, both good and bad, and therefore one must surprise the customer in terms of service in order to achieve an edge.'

The present programme began in 1988, but as early as 1983 the English and Welsh branches of the Royal Bank of Scotland (then operating separately as Williams and Glyn's Bank) introduced a 'Code of Customer Service'. This was a 'written statement of the bank's policy, attitudes and intentions in its relationship with its customers,' as *Newsline*, the company's internal magazine, described it. However, in 1985 the clearing-bank operations underwent radical reorganisation when the two banks merged under the Royal Bank of Scotland umbrella. The developments taking place at the time failed to place enough emphasis on the 'code', which consequently fell into disuse.

After the dust had settled, the bank decided that it had to increase its competitive edge in order to survive. It started with the introduction of service circles in 1985, and in early 1987 management asked the training department to draw up plans for a customer-service programme. Top management rejected the initial proposals for not being ambitious enough.

In conjunction with an external consultant, Human Resource Development Ltd, the bank's training department conducted a customer-service audit in autumn 1987. The study concluded that a major obstacle to any programme lay in the bank's organisational climate. Employees needed an open, consultative, informative style of leadership where their enthusiasm and opinions would be welcomed, not the auto-cratic management style then in place. The programme's insti-gators decided that in order for their plans to succeed, they had to concentrate on management issues and uniting the workforce.

Implementing the Programme

The training department devised a two-year company-wide programme called 'Where People Matter'. This involved a series of one-day courses for all employees and a series of three-day courses for managerial staff, including senior man-agement. The courses began in February 1988 and were com-pleted in December 1989, covering a total of fifteen months, involving over 20,000 staff on 950 course programmes and costing £2.5 million.

Crawford explains, 'The objective of the one-day course was to create an awareness among staff of the bank's customers, both internal and external, and their needs.' Participants met in groups of thirty for formal presentations, and then divided into groups of six for discussion and syndicate work. The groups comprised a mix of ranks and experience in order to help break down communication barriers between managers and staff and between different departments.

The three-day management course met in groups of twelve and introduced people to two workplace activities, 'Surprising the Customer' and 'Doing It Right', around which the course was based. The former examined three service methods employed by the bank: service in person, on the telephone and in writing. For these methods to be effective, the bank had to give a service that the customer would remember as a pleasant experience, and the course suggested words and deeds to help accomplish this.

'Doing It Right' looked at the bank's services 'from the point of view of what to do and how to do it,' as Crawford puts it. 'Staff were asked to consider how the bank should carry out its services from the perspective of the customer to establish new standards of performance.'

Both sessions aimed to develop the key communication skills necessary to ensure that standards of performance and workplace activities were agreed, implemented and monitored. Says Crawford: 'The whole success of the programme depended on managers' involvement and communication with the staff, and therefore the course was designed to impact on their style of leadership by developing their influence skills, such as goal setting, joining forces, persuasion and assertiveness.'

The formal courses were intended only as a precursor to the long-term programme, where top management hoped to develop the motivation and enthusiasm of employees. They planned to keep the momentum going locally through focused quality circles, comprising a group of volunteers from each branch who would meet regularly to discuss various aspects of service.

Originally introduced as a support mechanism for the 'Code of Customer Service', the quality circles had suffered the same fate as the 'Code', only to be reintroduced throughout the branches early in 1986. However, the idea of quality circles failed to gain general acceptance at that time, according to Crawford, because of the choice of the 'cascade', or top-down, form of communication, with each level of management introducing the concept to their subordinates. 'The message tended to get distorted by the time it got to the bottom,' says Crawford. 'To overcome that, we started to use a prepared script. But that didn't work either, as it often appeared forced and unnatural.' The 1987 customer-service audit had found that quality circles worked only when managers were committed to the concept and got involved themselves, responding positively and promptly to suggestions made by the circles' members.

As part of the new programme, the bank set about redirecting the operation of quality circles (now called service circles) and providing more structure for them. The form of the circles did not change dramatically: they still consist of four to eight volunteers, are chaired by a leader of their own choice and deal with issues relevant to their particular workplace. They discuss what customers require and make recommendations to management. What did change, however, was that service circles now form part of a team effort with management. The basic aim, to improve service, is aided by a standardised process of analysis:

1. Look at and identify the current situation; observe but do not judge

2. Identify what the customer requires

3. Identify the gap between what is provided and what is desired

4. Gather ideas for improvements

5. Present the ideas to management

6. Implement action

7. Set service standards

This last point – setting service standards – is one of the most important aspects of a service circle's role. As Crawford explains: 'Here the question of ownership is paramount. If standards are simply handed down by management, the staff will be much less committed to them than if they themselves are involved in the design and implementation . . . For the future of the bank, the service circles will lead the way in the quest to improve overall standards within the organisation.'

Effects of the Programme

Crawford points to the creation of a new organisational climate at the bank as a major result of the programme. 'It can be described by the Japanese term *"kaizen"*, meaning an attitude of mind geared towards improvement. The bank's employees are not sitting on their laurels but are striving to increase the levels of service to even greater heights.'

Internal communications have also benefited from the programme. Managers have a greater awareness of the enthusiasm and energy that exist among staff, and the company magazine, *Newsline*, spreads the news about the success of the service circles. 'Where People Matter' has improved job satisfaction and interpersonal skills are now one of the important criteria when hiring new staff.

The bottom line, of course, is the profitability of the company. Crawford comments: 'Increased profits and good customer-service standards go hand in hand, and since the Royal Bank's profit levels are steadily increasing, it would be fair to say that improved customer services have been a contributory factor in this achievement.'

The programme has not been without its problems, however. All innovations will attract adverse criticism from cynics and the bank's programme was no exception. While the cynics were in the minority by far, they did tend to be at middle-management level. The 1987 audit had anticipated some resistance, of course, and the training department designed the programme to surmount this difficulty. As Crawford says:

> Of course, you can't win the hearts of all the people all the time. But we have worked to overcome some of that cynicism by focusing more on management training. For example, managers now attend a four-day training programme (as opposed to a one-day programme for clerical staff). We find it helps to have a wide range of attendees – with everyone from the most senior to the most junior managers together on the same training programme. They learn from each other.

Advice to Other Companies

The Royal Bank believes that service circles are the optimum vehicle for tapping that invaluable resource – the staff. Over six years of both failure and success with such circles, it has identified seven crucial elements necessary in their design:

1. They must be introduced as part of a wider campaign to improve customer service

2. Membership must be voluntary

3. They must focus exclusively on customer service

4. They must be action-centred – not just a talking shop

5. Management must be involved and committed

6. Management must respond positively to suggestions

7. A simple process must be designed to aid discussion and analysis of any problems

Crawford's final advice is twofold. First, an organisation must always ask itself why it is performing a certain function; if the answer is not for the benefit of the customer, then it is wasting energy and resources. Second, never assume the company is better than it really is. 'There is always room for improvement in all areas of an organisation's activities, especially customer service. As the saying goes, "You don't have to be sick to get better."'

19

WOOLWICH BUILDING
SOCIETY

The recent upheaval in the financial sector has forced both banks and building societies to recognise the need for greater customer care.

Building societies, once the dominant players in the home-loans and personal-savings markets, were driven out of their complacency in the early 1980s. Legislative changes in 1981 brought banks into the home-mortgage market, while the Building Societies Act of 1986 allowed building societies to offer a wider range of products and services, putting them for the first time in direct competition with the banks. At the same time, new taxes on profits on the sales of government stock forced building societies to rely on mortgage lending more and more to stay profitable.

All these factors have made for a more competitive atmosphere. As Woolwich Building Society Chief Executive Donald Kirkham said in his address to the 1986 management conference:

> Until a few years ago, we, the Woolwich, played our game under relatively genteel conditions against just the other building societies, because no one else wanted to come on to our playing field. Then, it didn't matter whether you won or lost but how you played the game. Yesterday, only growth was at stake. Today, it's a matter of survival.

The Woolwich's challenge at this point was to convince its staff that they were entering a new business world, one increasingly influenced by the need to put the customer first.

Kirkham, inspired by the film of the book *In Search of Excellence*, asked Woolwich Training and Development Manager Bernard Wynne to 'gather a team of committed people to translate the abstract ideas of the film into positive action'.

Wynne, with the help of David Blake and Jackie Riley, the assistant general managers responsible for corporate affairs and corporate planning respectively, departmental manager Ron Walpole, assistant general manager for marketing Huw Alderman and an area manager for branches, Bob Chapman, formed the campaign executive, under Blake's chairmanship, to implement the customer-care programme. Hilary McVitty, the Woolwich's customer-relations controller, became the campaign's full-time coordinator.

Implementing the Programme

Between March and September 1986 the campaign executive carried out a major survey about the programme and about feelings towards the Woolwich. This was entirely conducted through visits and meetings with groups of employees.

The results were not promising. 'The sheer number of problems coming out seemed overwhelming,' says Blake. 'Most of the problems focused on pure bureaucracy or a preponderance of "irksome tasks", such as customer assistants having to ask a manager for a password before they could gain computer access. Some staff felt that training did not concentrate on customer service, but on administrative issues.'

However, the results did show a good deal of loyalty and motivation among all levels of staff and most said they saw their jobs as more than just a way of making a living. They saw customers as people. Blake believes this stems from the

Woolwich's long-standing belief that it was 'in the people business'.

There was, none the less, some initial resistance to a customer-care programme, primarily from longer-serving staff and senior management outside the executive. 'Some of the older managers thought that the programme would not help, or that the Woolwich didn't need it. Our younger staff were much more enthusiastic,' says Blake.

The biggest obstacle, according to Blake, was a feeling among some staff that they 'had heard it all before', and a belief that the changes might not last. 'The biggest plus,' he says, 'was the complete commitment of Chief Executive Donald Kirkham and the senior executive team.'

Customers can also be cynical and suspicious of what could appear to be superficial friendliness, says Blake: 'The British public don't like artificiality, so sometimes the pleasantness of staff might be misinterpreted. They may also dislike overtly positive responses from sales staff because they don't necessarily want to be sold anything.'

Clearly, the customer-care programme called for far more than a smile campaign: the Woolwich was looking at a fundamental change in the way it did business. Kirkham outlined the specifics at the 1986 management conference in Eastbourne. The campaign – called 'Striving for Excellence' – plan involved:

- an educational programme for all staff

- a one-day executive course and a two-day senior manager course using external consultants

- two-day courses at various venues, run by Woolwich training staff for other managers, supervisors and staff

- surveys of customers and staff

- a staff-suggestion scheme

- awards to recognise individual excellence

- staff appraisals with greater emphasis on intangible aspects of service, such as smiles and approachability

- campaign logos, video and audio cassettes, staff bulletins and corporate wear (uniforms)

Together, these factors were designed to create a greater awareness of customer service, an aspiration to excellence in all areas and a culture that promoted serving the internal as well as the external customer. One of the more specific goals was to provide borrowers with the kind of customer care that investors had come to expect.

One of the early steps to help underline the priorities in frontline jobs was a change from the title of cashier to customer assistant. Two further initiatives helped cut through the tradition of bureaucracy: the practice of MBWA (Management By Walking About), a system through which managers speak to both customers and staff directly, and a suggestion-scheme called 'Bright Ideas'. By November 1988 'Bright Ideas' had received over 1,200 suggestions, one of which saved the society over £40,000 on its yearly lighting bill.

The Woolwich has also tried to achieve what it calls a FAME image (Friendly and Approachable, Modern and Effective). The modern and effective image relates to the physical presentation of the Woolwich to the outside world, including corporate wear – and physical improvements to the branches, such as the introduction of inquiry desks in some of the larger ones.

To support these initiatives, the Woolwich launched an intensive, three-tier staff-training programme. Until 1986, staff training had included very little in the way of customer care. Instead, says Blake, 'People tended to rely on their common sense.' Now, all staff, except top-level management, attend a two-day residential course. Called 'People Business', it deals with the concepts of internal and external customers and the importance of customer service to the society's future. The 'Excellent Leader' course, designed for the top 120 managers, concentrates on leadership skills and objectives, while another course for middle managers focuses on both leadership and customer service skills.

Effects of the Programme

The customer-care programme has had a measurable impact on staff attitudes. In 1986, 82 per cent of staff rated Woolwich's service as 'good' and 4 per cent rated it as 'excellent'. In 1988 the figures were 83 and 9 per cent respectively. In the original survey, staff rated the Woolwich most effective when it came to helpful and friendly staff, efficient staff and competitive interest rates, and these ratings all improved in the 1988 survey. Employees gave the Woolwich poor marks on questions of additional terminals in branches away from cashiers and sufficient staff at busy times and branch inquiry desks, but even these ratings improved in the 1988 survey. Overall, staff said they had seen substantial improvements in customer service and internal communications, especially in terms of channels available to relay suggestions to management. They also felt the 'Bright Ideas' scheme was having an effect.

Borrowers came out particularly well. In 1988 three out of five employees said that the Woolwich offered borrowers and investors the same level of service, while two in five employees said that services to the borrower were now better.

One of the most telling results, however, was the way respondents — both customers and staff — ranked the Woolwich's service relative to the competition. In 1986 staff were far more critical of the level of service provided by the Woolwich in comparison with its customers. As far as customers were concerned, just over a quarter rated the service as excellent, with the vast majority of the remainder rating it as good. Staff were much more critical, with only 4 per cent thinking the service excellent and just over 10 per cent even suggesting it was poor or very poor. By 1988 many more customers rated the Woolwich's service as excellent and the number of staff rating it excellent doubled, while the numbers saying poor or very poor halved.

Of course, the overall winners have been the customers. Had the banks and building societies not been thrown into direct competition, perhaps customer care would never have reached high-street financial institutions. After all, there had been little overt pressure from the public to change. As Blake says: 'The British do not complain, but they do translate dissatisfaction directly to action. They will close their accounts, saying nothing – and, of course, you will never know why they closed their accounts. Now, perhaps, customers have the option of opening accounts on the basis of service.'

20

WOOLWORTHS

Woolworths entered the 1980s in a sorry state. It may have had over 1,000 stores to its name, but many of these were in areas of declining population and others were in the invidious position of competing with sister stores. No one knew exactly how many merchandise lines there were, but estimates put the figure at over 50,000. Stocks were valued at over half of turnover and sales information was non-existent. Woolworths had a poor high-street image. The management hierarchy was top-heavy and staff morale was low. With a profile like this, it should have come as no surprise that in 1982 the company made a loss of over £5 million.

What had led Woolworths to this sad state of affairs? According to a spokesman for the company, 'The business was too complicated and bureaucratic. It was not able to respond to consumer demands quickly enough, when retail concepts were changing rapidly and customer expectations with them.'

Against this background of disenchantment, Paternoster Stores paid £310 million for the ailing company in a 1982 management buyout. During 1983, under the new name Woolworths Holdings plc, the new management developed a turnaround strategy. Today the holding company, now known as Kingfisher plc, comprises Woolworths, B&Q, Comet, Superdrug, Chartwell Land and Charlie Browns.

John Beckett, who headed up the turnaround team, feels

that the problems Woolworths had went back to a time well before the outgoing board:

> The tradition of Woolworths was to sell very large numbers of small items at 3d or 6d each. That was the basis of the business and it provided a focus not only for the manager and the buyer but throughout the organisation. When they removed that discipline the company began to lose its focus, both with the customers and with the employees.

'Operation Focus'

Research identified two types of Woolworths store: approximately 200 larger 'comparison' stores in highly competitive high streets and about 600 smaller 'convenience' stores in secondary locations. A further 200 sites were closed as unprofitable ventures.

Overhauling the chain involved a number of parallel strategies: disposal of low-profit units with least potential, separate formats for the two types of store and rationalisation of store size. Most important of all, Woolworths focused on fewer departments in order to reposition itself as a specialist in key areas and improve the profit per square foot of selling space.

To identify the key areas, top management looked for markets with growth potential where the company already had a meaningful share and sufficient credibility to compete successfully. After extensive market research, it developed five 'focus' areas: 'Kidswear'; 'Toys & Stationery'; 'Music & Video', including videos, records, cassettes and accessories; 'Gifts & Sweets'; and 'Home Essentials', comprising garden and kitchen goods, DIY, horticulture and appliances. It dropped two large areas, food and adult clothing, thus freeing up around 1 million square feet of extra selling space for the 'focus' merchandise.

Initial testing of the 'focus' strategy showed that despite the withdrawal of some 20,000 product lines, 68 per cent of customers believed there to be a wide range of goods for sale. In the larger stores, the average spend increased by 65 per cent and profit per square foot increased dramatically. Encouraged by these results, the company implemented the strategy throughout the chain.

An exercise of this magnitude requires considerable human resources, and over the last three years Woolworths has recruited specialists to build powerful marketing and merchandising teams in each 'focus' area. In July 1987, in order to monitor performance by area better, it made each a separate profit centre.

The results of 'Operation Focus' have been impressive. The 1982 loss of £5 million was transformed into a profit of £55 million for the 1988–9 financial year. Woolworths also holds a dominant market position in three of its five key areas.

Rationalisation of unprofitable businesses and improved service levels are the key elements of the successful turnaround strategy. Though the latter has not involved a customer-care programme, ' "Focus" is an attempt at satisfying customers' needs in a vastly improved environment,' said a spokesman for the company.

Improving Customer Service

How has Woolworths gone about transforming its service to customers? An extensive refurbishment programme of its 200 high-street stores has played a part, as has the investment of some £5.5 million each year on training its 27,000 employees.

The commitment to training starts at the top, says Personnel Director Leo McKee: 'The contribution of our employees is crucial to our success. Training is vital as we have to ensure that our staff at all levels are equipped to meet the challenges of an increasingly competitive retail environment. Much of that training is now organised in-house and is tailored to meet individual needs.'

In July 1987 Woolworths adopted an 'excellence' training programme. This aims to make sales assistants fully proficient and more confident when dealing with customers. The programme rewards staff for their achievements and their progress towards standards of personal and team excellence. The programme laid the foundation for improved product knowledge and standards of customer care among staff. The same year it introduced uniforms with pockets. This was a small change but the indication of trust was a positive morale boost.

Woolworths also started an annual profit-sharing scheme for all store and administration staff. In the first year, 1987, it paid out £1.5 million in bonuses and offered the first share option scheme, enabling the staff to benefit directly from the company's improved financial health. 'Woolworths recognises that our success has been achieved through a commitment to teamwork, and this scheme ensures that staff share in that success,' said a spokesman.

The organisation has created a more structured career path and actively encourages internal promotions for employees with managerial ability and leadership potential. Says McKee: 'Our aim is for everyone in Woolworths to have the opportunity to develop his or her career. Our dynamic business encourages high-fliers to stay and make a long-term career commitment to Woolworths. Moreover, we can offer exciting opportunities for people coming into the business and are able to attract new recruits of the highest calibre.'

Obstacles and Problems

Poor-quality products and the non-delivery or late-delivery of orders caused difficulties in meeting customer needs. To combat these problems, Woolworths has upgraded its three quality-control laboratories, where products are tested, and has reduced the number of delivery centres to just two, operating on a just-in-time basis. Distribution has improved dramatically as a result.

The Future

Woolworths' strategy for 1988–9 was threefold:

1. To establish category leadership in large, attractive markets with long-term growth potential

2. To achieve operational excellence and high standards of customer care

3. To maintain the growth and financial success of the business by exploiting opportunities and managing costs

Looking ahead, the company sees the tough and competitive retail climate continuing, with customers becoming ever more demanding and value-oriented. The future will see Woolworths continuing to focus on its five key areas and on the motivation and development of its staff. 'Our aim is to be recognised as *the* specialist high-street retailer supplying the needs of today's young families.'

Appendix I

CUSTOMER-CARE SURVEY

Summary and Highlights of Customer-Care Questionnaire

The ITEM Group's survey of companies implementing customer-care programmes indicates more positive experience than previous observations, but highlights a number of significant problems which reduce the effectiveness of companies' efforts.
  In particular:

- 20% of companies did not set measurable objectives for their programmes, and slightly more failed to set objectives for the training element of their programmes.

- Training was relatively superficial in most cases, amounting to two days or less in two-thirds of companies (and less than a half-day in 18%).

- Only just over two-thirds of companies applied quantifiable measurements to test the effectiveness of their training.

- Only 40% of programmes involved training in customer-oriented leadership.

- Only 27% trained top management.

- Only 43% gave employees authority to deal with customer-care problems, although another 49% did so 'sometimes'.

- 45% of companies report that their employees saw the programme as 'flavour of the month'; 36% viewed it with suspicion. However, 42% said employees perceived it as a genuine and welcome change of orientation.

- Only 21% of programmes have fully met their objectives, although 40% have mostly done so.

- Just over 50% of companies are into a 'next stage' of customer-care; 11% have reached a plateau; 8% have lost impetus after an initial flush of enthusiasm and 29% 'are only just appreciating how much more there is to do'.

Customer-Care Questionnaire

General

The ITEM Group's customer-care questionnaire was sent to 1,000 major UK companies, of which 75 replied. Their responses are outlined below.

Does your company have a customer-care and/or quality training initiative?

85% of those who responded said they *did* have such an initiative.
90% of those who *did not* have such an initiative said they planned to implement one.

When was the initiative/will it be launched?

1986:	4%	1987:	6%	1988:	23%
1989:	31%	1990:	30%	1991:	6%

Preparation

What preparation was/will be made for the programme?

customer survey(s)/market research	73%
employee attitude survey(s)	67%
articles in company publications	63%
cascade briefings	60%

Other preparation included consultation with line and senior management; brief video training sessions; and staff presentations conducted by the board of directors.

Did/has the company set specific objectives for the programme?

Yes 71%
No 29%

Specific objectives included identifying what customers expected from: the company's employees; its facilities; and its services. Some respondents placed emphasis on the importance of the customer to the business now and in the future, and on exceeding customer expectations.

Did you set specific and measurable objectives for the training element of the initiative?

Yes 66%
No 34%

Who was/will the programme be aimed at?

all employees	85%
front line staff	21%
non-management employees	7%
management only	7%

Some companies also suggested training should be aimed at contractors, to ensure maximum customer care at all levels.

What form did/will the training take?

awareness sessions on site	62%
awareness sessions away from the workplace	45%
full training programme	73%
distance learning	7%

Training in telephone techniques was also mentioned.

How long do/ will training sessions run in total per employee?

half a day or less	18%
half a day to one day	21%
one to two days	27%
two to five days	30%
more than five days	4%

How have you measured/will you evaluate results against the training objectives?

through specific, quantifiable measurements	42%
through qualitative measurements	39%
no system of measurement	19%

Other means of measurement included market research questionnaires, the increase in business generated and the drop in the number of complaints.

What subject matter did/will the training cover?

creating awareness	89%
changing attitudes	89%
changing behaviours	79%
training in customer handling skills	75%
training in problem-solving skills	52%
training in customer-oriented leadership	38%
training in team skills	48%
creating quality processes and systems of working	43%
management development	27%

Some companies also used video situation roleplays; training in the effective use of statistics; benchmarking, and 'spiritual' development.

Implementation

Who led/will lead these sessions?

internal trainer(s)	53%
internal line managers	51%
external consultant(s)	36%
external consultant initially, then internal people after a 'train the trainer' programme	45%

Did the initiative cover any other type of activity?

a review of structures	33%
a review of systems	51%
a staff suggestion scheme	36%
a system for celebrating success	27%
a review of reward systems, financial and non-financial	18%
a culture review	41%
top management training	27%

Only one company mentioned any other type of activity, which included publications in the company newsletter, and presentations to management.

How were/will the sessions be supported?

demonstrated presence and commitment from top management	89%
explanatory materials	67%
personnel workbooks, action assignments, etc	49%
video/audio support material, etc	59%
visits to/by customers	38%

Were/will each group of participants encouraged/be encouraged immediately to start work on specific customer-care problems?

Yes 85%
No   15%

Were they/will they be given authority to deal with these problems?

Yes   43%
No   8%
Sometimes 49%

Results (answered only by companies which already have programmes)

Overall did employees initially –

see the programmes as 'flavour of the month'? 45%
perceive it as a genuine and welcome change of
    orientation?   42%
view it with suspicion?   36%
have no preconceptions?   10%

Has your programme fulfilled the objectives you set?

fully   2%
mostly   40%
only to a small degree   6%
not at all   2%
we didn't set measurable objectives/haven't
    measured   11%
too early to say   39%

Has the training fulfilled the objectives you set?

fully	7%
mostly	46%
only to a small degree	5%
not at all	0%
we didn't set measurable objectives/haven't measured	10%
too early to say	32%

Which of the following statements best describes your situation now?

we have done all we need to in customer care	0%
we have achieved our initial objectives and are now into a further stage of customer-care development	52%
the initial programme was reasonably successful but we are now at a plateau	11%
after an initial flush of enthusiasm, the impetus has been lost	8%
we are only just appreciating how much more there is to do	29%

Some companies felt the need to relaunch their customer-care programme and others felt it required a more focused approach.

Given the opportunity, what would you do differently?

Many respondents expressed the opinion that they would ensure the full commitment and awareness of senior and line management, in enforcing new strategies after training sessions. They felt initial planning was inadequate to facilitate the organisational changes necessary, and that all programmes should be developed with follow-up strategies.

In the production industry more time was required to carry out practical and operational restructuring at shop floor level.

How do you see the process developing?

Initial schemes seem likely to develop much further, along with the introduction of Total Quality Management programmes, with further quality training aimed at creating greater enthusiasm, more team spirit, and greater customer awareness for internal and external customers. Many companies will aim for better direction and focus, with more positive reinforcement of techniques until the various programmes become integrated into the company culture. Most companies acknowledged that improvement in the quality of service is continuous through the development of the programme.

As senior and line managers are now becoming more convinced of the effectiveness of customer-care and quality training initiatives, some companies are finding the need to create local customer-care teams as a focal point to assist managers in developing initiatives and measuring success in maintaining the philosophy of customer care at local level.

Appendix II

HOW TO OBTAIN
CUSTOMER-SERVICE FEEDBACK

What do we need to know?

1. What are our customers' service needs?
2. How well are we meeting them?
   (a) What do we do well?
   (b) What do we do badly?
3. Where could we create competitive advantage through service?

Who should we ask?

1. A cross-section of current customers
2. A selection of past and potential customers
3. Employees
4. Anyone who can throw light on the issues

What methods should we use?

1. Informal listening and discussions
2. Focus groups

3. Postal surveys
4. Telephone surveys
5. Formal customer visits
6. Open days
7. Encouraging complaints

Who should be involved?

1. Everyone in the company
2. Suppliers, agents and distributors

How will we use the information?

1. What improvements do we need to make?
2. Can several problems be aggregated into a larger one?
3. Is there potential for competitive advantage?

BIBLIOGRAPHY

Blanchard, Kenneth and Lorber, Robert, *Putting the One-Minute Manager to Work*, Willow Books, 1983

Blanchard, Kenneth, *The One-Minute Manager*, Willow Books, 1981

Goldsmith, Walter and Clutterbuck, David, *The Winning Streak: Britain's top companies reveal their formulas for success*, Weidenfeld and Nicolson, 1984

Foster, Geoffrey, 'Kwik-Fit's Fast Reflex', *Management Today*, December 1986

On Achieving Excellence, Vol. 4 No. 8, August 1989

'Organize to Create Customer Value', The Boston Consulting Group, 1987

'Personnel Management Fact Sheet', *Personnel Management*, January 1989

Peters, Thomas J. and Waterman, Robert H., *In Search of Excellence: lessons from America's best-run companies*, Harper and Row, 1982

'Survey of Clearing Banks', *What To Buy for Business*, No. 89, August 1988

INDEX